Capture Your Dream

Capture Your Dream

Stack Real-World Goals
Develop Your Dragons
Thrive Beyond the 9 to 5

By Sandy Lender

IYF Publishing/Dragon Hoard Press

This publication is designed to offer authoritative, inspirational, and motivational information regarding the subject. Neither the publisher nor author are engaged in rendering accounting, legal, or other professional services. Nothing herein creates an attorney-client relationship. Nothing herein constitutes legal advice or a solicitation to offer legal advice. If the reader requires legal or other expert assistance, the services of professional counsel should be sought.

Published by IYF/Dragon Hoard Press, Florida
www.SandyLenderInk.com

Copyright © 2025 Sandy Lender Ink

All rights reserved.
No part of this book may be reproduced, stored in or introduced into a retrieval system, or transmitted, in any form, or by any means (electronic, mechanical, photocopying, recording, or otherwise), without the prior permission of the publisher. Any web addresses or links referenced in this book were live and correct at the time of the book's publication but may be subject to change.

Lender, Sandy
Capture Your Dream : Stack Real-World Goals, Develop Your Dragons, Thrive Beyond the 9 to 5 / Sandy Lender – First edition.

Cover design: Sandy Lender
Dragon illustration: Solomandra
Editors: Stephen Zimmer, Jen Selinsky
This book is the intellectual property of the author, Sandy Lender, and none of it was generated via artificial intelligence.
Paperback ISBN: 979-8-9909082-4-6
eBook ISBN: 979-8-9909082-5-3

DEDICATION

I dedicate this book to Amanda Chariss.
Thank you for focusing the dream
all those years ago.

CONTENTS

Foreword by Kimberly Hoffman — ix
Acknowledgments — xi
Introspection & How to Use This Book — xiii

Part One: We All Have a Why

1 – Dragon Mottos vs Daring Mistakes — 23
2 – Lessons from a Kid's Dreams Turned to Realism — 33
3 – Conquer the First Few Monsters — 43
4 – A.J. Takes on an Asphalt Monster — 59
5 – Bryce Fixes All the Monsters — 67

Part Two: Let's Start Building

6 – Embrace the Dragon of Change — 77
7 – Exercises for Dreaming Your Career into Being — 89
8 – You're Not in This Alone — 111
9 – Capture the Dream in the Real World — 135
10 – Assess Your Dragon Score — 145
11 – Give Yourself Permission to Pivot — 157

Notes & Diffusing Your "Why" — 165
About the Author — 172

FOREWORD

How do you follow your dreams? Do you have the right skills, financial assets, and passion to reach your goals? *Capture Your Dream* dives into these questions and helps you find your dragons that carry you through and the monsters that try to stop you, so that you can find the path to achieve your goals and dreams.

Author Sandy Lender is an amazing author, mentor, and friend. I met Sandy several years ago at the Imaginarium Conference. Her kind and gentle spirit, yet with a warrior's heart, encouraged me and helped me as I was seeking to fulfill my dreams. Sandy lives out her faith through her life and her writing and I'm blessed to know her.

As you will discover in this book, Sandy's side hustle is writing. Writing is my side hustle as well. I work a 40-hour-a-week job in the diesel engine business while writing children's books on the side. To fuel my passion at work, I have found opportunities to write for an employee resource group on the topic of disability inclusion in our quarterly newsletter. But my heart's passion is writing amazing stories for children that help them see that they can overcome, be kind, see their worth, and know they are loved.

The company where I am employed allows me to flex my hours so that I can speak at schools and civic clubs in the surrounding communities. I set goals, eliminate distractions, and set aside the time to reach my goals with regards to my writing. It's not easy as I sometimes encounter roadblocks due to my disability, time, or other commitments. But I use my dragon to get back on course.

Sandy writes from her heart and from experience. She lays out in easy-to-understand text how you can achieve your goals even when it's not your main gig. There are many of us out there who have a passion that we are working to launch into a full-time career, but we are not there yet.

So, we are side hustling. We are waiting for the day when it becomes the main gig, but even if it doesn't, we can use the plans laid out in this book to keep pursuing our passion.

My prayer for you is that as you read this amazing book you find your dragon and eliminate the monsters that will keep you from reaching your goals.

In pursuit of my dreams,
Kimberly S. Hoffman, Author/Speaker
https://kimberlyhoffmanblog.wordpress.com/

ACKNOWLEDGMENTS

First and foremost, I must thank my Lord and Savior, Jesus Christ, for getting me through each day. When I remember to seek His guidance, I have a much better chance at achieving the goals I set in place.

Thank you Tom Kuennen, Jay Winford, John Ball, for taking the time to read and speak kindly about *Capture Your Dream* before it even saw the light of day. Your support means more than you know.

I also want to thank a specific set of businesspeople and creatives who stepped into my process and helped me bring this book together:

Kimberly Hoffman, there are many friendships formed at the Imaginarium Convention, and I count yours among the most dear. What a privilege it is to know a woman with a compassionate heart like yours and to count that woman as a friend. Thank you for writing a foreword with such thoughtfulness and kindness.

Lennie Loesch, thank you for taking the time out of what I know is a rigorous schedule to read this book's second draft and literally redline items. Your guidance and ideas over the past twenty-plus years have always been valuable to me and this project was one more reminder of how much wisdom you have to share.

Ed Wallace, you were so kind to read through the first draft of *Capture Your Dream* and identify areas that needed expansion and those that needed trimming. Your wisdom and kindness are truly appreciated. Thank you for the phone call and your patience while I scribbled notes.

A.J. Ronyak, your friendship over the past twenty-five years has been a hoot! It was a delight to review your story and share with readers how you developed your side hustle to the benefit of an entire industry. Thank you for sharing the Scrapbook of Awesomeness.

Bryce Wuori, thank you for letting your vulnerability and strength shine through for readers' benefit. It was a pleasure to visit with you about your highs and lows and I appreciate you sharing your path for *Capture Your Dream*.

Cara Owings, thank you for sharing your story amid all the busy times we've had this past year. I don't think I told you that I'm in awe of all you've accomplished; you embody the concept of collaboration in pursuit of the side hustle.

Stephen Zimmer and Jen Zelinsky, the two of you are dear friends and colleagues in this writing endeavor and I thank you for the wordsmithing help. (And for the Duran Duran conversations.)

I would also like to thank all my far-away friends, family, and colleagues for help and inspiration to achieve the day job alongside the side hustle that keeps me rolling out of bed early in the morning...

INTROSPECTION

After thirty-two years in the publishing business, I'm using the commotion around the artificial intelligence (AI) disruption as an excuse for introspection.

Over these three-plus decades, I've applied the truths in *Who Moved My Cheese* by Dr. Spencer Johnson to my career and made Andrew Groves' *Only the Paranoid Survive* a motto for my life. I've internalized the neurology of free will from Charles Duhigg's *The Power of Habit*, and I've tried my best to emulate the ideas from *The Leadership Wisdom of Jesus* by Charles C. Manz.

Even books that didn't resonate fully with me, like *Blue Ocean Strategy*, still contained nuggets of wisdom to guide me through some passage of my professional career. For example, I don't have a wingman supporting me in my magazine publishing career or my author side hustle, but I can take the motivations and detail-talk from Lt. Col. Rob "Waldo" Waldman's *Never Fly Solo* to heart.

The introspection and deep thinking I've applied to my career and my circumstances, such as attending a keynote address by Daymond John of Shark Tank fame, or reading Anne Lamont's *Bird by Bird*, aren't the same as what I'm referring to when it comes to

> **I'm going to admit to, and allow you to learn from, mistakes I've made.**

considering the disruption taking place in the publishing industry today. The number of colleagues I see jumping on the bandwagon to let AI generate content for their magazines, websites, book covers, and even book content disturbs me as a creative who enjoys the writing side of the editor-in-chief's job.

For example, more than one competing organization of *AsphaltPro* Magazine, for which I have been the editor since its inception in 2007, has used AI to take from my company's website content my employer paid me to create. The entities have used that content in aggregate-source e-newsletters to generate revenue for themselves. One of those companies recently used a broken link; I assume because no human was double-checking the AI before e-blasting the stolen material to their audience.

There are good and useful ways to employ AI tools without taking intellectual property others have not authorized one to use.

I consider that unethical, lazy, and an example of poor quality control. There are good and useful ways to employ AI tools without taking intellectual property others have not authorized one to use. In chapter eight, we'll talk specifically about using your own material to build an AI assistant without trouncing upon anyone's copyright.

As we dive into this book that acknowledges the importance of growing a career in the real world while nurturing the side hustle that satisfies your dreams, I'll talk at length about the writing side of my life, and you'll come to see why it astounds me to think anyone would allow the skill to atrophy in favor of giving our creative endeavors to a computer's mind instead of our own.

As I'm typing this introduction, Bloom Books has pulled the AI-generated covers for Sophie Lark's *Grimstone* and *Monarch* to reproduce them with human artists, and I applaud not only the reading community's outcry at the covers, but also the publisher's swift action in rectifying an initial error in judgment.

Let me hurry to set the tech bros at ease: I don't condemn **all** AI use.

There is value in handing off to a learning program our repetitive, mindless tasks that would typically involve hours of pouring over data to analyze audience spending habits or to figure out what inventory to purchase for restocking a specific seasonal product. But I revile the idea we should let a learning machine do our creative thought processes under the guise of making business faster. Isn't that concept why no one can make an emergency phone call to a loved one from a stranger's phone?

We're dooming ourselves to be useless idiots without soul or creativity if we let the AI do the fun stuff like developing art, clever headlines, interview questions, novels, poetry, short stories, and other works that require the human heart.

LET'S VEER BACK TO THE "BUSINESS" TOPIC
As I've watched competitors allow AI to seep into and downgrade the quality of work they churn out, I've considered how technology shifts and changes our jobs and careers throughout our lives. I've looked also at the way our economic upheaval — since the COVID-19 situation and closing of strategic infrastructure developments in North America — has exacerbated financial unease for new adults seeking fulfilling employment in a career they'd hoped would bring them joy and a sustainable lifestyle.

I've factored in how we, as humans in this journey together, can accept the reality of "workin' for a livin'," as the fabulous Huey Lewis and The News sang for us in 1982, while achieving a dream job for which our educational system might or might not have prepared us.

In this book, I offer real-world examples from my career in magazine and newsletter publishing since 1992. I also provide real-world examples from my side hustle as a bestselling poet and award-winning author who has worked with multiple independent publishing houses. And I showcase real-world examples from select businesspersons who have nurtured successful side hustles, as well. The day job isn't all we have in this life. There's more to living than working unpaid overtime for a 9-5 and collapsing onto your bed when you get home.

> **The day job isn't all we have in this life.**

HOW TO USE THIS BOOK

You'll notice a conversational style throughout the book. I'm talking to you as a friend and a colleague, not as a CEO from on high.

It might surprise you to find this in a motivational business book, but I'm going to admit to, and allow you to learn from, mistakes I've made. Of course, I'll also share with you successes, from myself and colleagues, that can offer guidance. This isn't your father's stodgy ol' business book with Venn diagrams and sales funnels. It's valid to feel emotions as you read through the anecdotes I present.

In the first part of this book, chapters one through five, I share some of the experiences and examples fellow entrepreneurs and I can provide to you through stories and ideas. The latter part, chapters six through eleven, gets more instructional with its examples and offers more to-do items, including tallying up your dragon score.

For readers who aren't familiar with my fiction, I write high fantasy — among other genres — and dragons factor heavily in the plots. It was only natural that these amazing creatures would help us chase our dreams.

Please don't picture cruel, menacing creatures reminiscent of Tolkien's reclusive Smaug; but instead imagine a variety of differently shaped and differently sized dragons full of wisdom and a desire to help humankind. We're going to explore the "good dragon" analogy of a critter to pursue and befriend for your best chance at achieving goals.

Chapter one explains further, and chapters nine and ten give you the opportunity to assess your current skills, potential skills, and typical goal-attacking strategies with your best dragon type. The exercises are offered in case you're thinking of switching careers, starting off after high school, or launching the "side" dream job.

Throughout these chapters, I'll interchange the concept of goals and dreams because I see the two as, quite often, interchangeable good dragons to chase down and capture. While we'll discuss how to set realistic goals to achieve a result — an overarching dream — much of what we're doing is reaching for an end goal. We're going for a dream we once cherished and might have forgotten.

My dear reader, let me help you remember!

Wherever you are in your journey, let me state right up front I'm proud of you for picking up this book and pouring hopeful information into your mind. That isn't toxic positivity, but true support.

I'm humbled you want to hear from my experiences, and I'm honored you would add what I've been through to your knowledge base going forward. I have a good feeling about you; I have a good feeling about your prospects. If you've taken the initiative to gather knowledge and grow your base, you're well on your way to setting and achieving goals that will increase your likelihood for success.

Let's get into this!

Thank you for reading,
Sandy Lender

PART ONE:
We All Have a Why

Chapter 1

Dragon Mottos vs Daring Mistakes

We live in the real world where adults must earn a living to survive. Of course, there's more to living than mere survival; there's more to living than showing up to the day job and logging in on a virtual time clock. Some of us have an entrepreneurial spirit or a well of creativity that begs us to follow a dream.

To make dreams come true in the real world, we need to set realistic goals according to our skills. There might be obstacles to overcome and monsters to slay, but the motivated dreamer is a force to be reckoned with. In fact, I suggest to you, motivated dreamers don't slay dragons; they seek them out and put them to work.

When Canadian author and blogger Douglas Gardham interviewed me in late 2023 for his podcast *Better Than Not*, he asked me about the motto I've used since 2006: "Some days, you just want the dragon to win." Elements from my answer will form several points for our discussion about how to find and build the skills we want to employ for a career that satisfies our dreams. I believe:

- we can chase goals on the side while working to survive;
- we can pursue a dream career; or
- we can blend those actions to realize a dream occupation.

Maybe it's the English major in me, but the symbolism of nurturing and rooting for the many "dragons" of encouragement, faith, mental and physical health and wellness, inspiration and motivation, on-the-job training, and perseverance, instead of treating them like monsters to be slain in their collective lair, appeals to me. As it has for many of my readers over the years, my speculative fiction slogan stood out to Doug. It caught his attention when I reached out to be a guest on his *Better Than Not* program using my tagline about rooting for the dragon in my email signature.

> **Discern which goals or steppingstones are helpful dragons to nurture and which are monsters to slay.**

Like Doug, I saw no harm in at least asking to try.

I'd been a guest on live and pre-recorded programs, other podcasts, blogs, and so on. Reaching out to a relatively new host who didn't focus on genre fiction specifically was out of my comfort zone, but I liked his conversational style of talking about creativity and life.

If he said, "No, we don't need you," it would've been no skin off my back. If he said, "Yes, let's schedule it," that would've been another opportunity to get my name in front of a new audience and meet a new author friend.

It was better to ask than not.

My spirit encapsulated exactly what Doug's podcast represented, and he said he appreciated that. My motto encapsulates the same idea: Some days, you're flipping the script and rooting for something no one else is rooting for.

"Some days, you just want the dragon to win" has different meanings for different circumstances. If we're talking in literal terms about fantasy creatures in genre fiction, then the slogan means exactly what it says. However, even then, we need to break it down.

- First, I tend to write clever, powerful, and wise-and-worthy dragons into my genre fiction because I can find the good in even a notoriously maligned creature. The worthy beast deserves to get the upper hand when fighting the cretins some human so-called "heroes" tend to be.
- Next, I recognize there *are* dragons who are the lesser of two evils in a story. If the dragon is the one who can — and is willing to — help a person fulfill a quest, but the self-important warrior sent to slay it would end up getting *you* killed in an upcoming battle, you better hope the dragon wins the day to become your powerful partner.

Let's use the dragon analogy as we go forward. I'm not going to suggest at any point in this motivational book you compromise your principles and partner with someone who is the lesser of two evils. I can give you an example of doing that and regretting it fully.

**SIDE-HUSTLING
WITH THE LESSER OF TWO EVILS**
In late 2012, I launched a print magazine with an individual whom I now believe to have been a predatory narcissist. We'll call

him Pal, which is obviously not his real name.

Pal was a self-proclaimed alcoholic. His inability to achieve sobriety put immense pressure on me to accomplish his load of the work, as well as mine, while we started a business, and I worked a full-time job.

I developed the business plan, found an investor to give us start-up capital, found a web design guru to get our site and email up and running, found a printer, learned the software to design and lay out the magazine, and began building our subscriber base, among other tasks necessary to launch a niche business-to-consumer publication.

Pal claimed to have had sales experience and was useful in talking to clients who refused to buy ads from a woman. Yes, that was during 2012, but I still had to direct certain clients to Pal based merely on chromosomes. However, those were not good reasons to align myself with him in starting a companion parrot magazine.

It's not always easy to recognize the dangerous people we'll run into in business until we're mired in a project with them, but I fully discourage choosing them if you can avoid it.

Learn from my lesson. That entailed five-plus years of working deep into the night while my partner slept off a pills-plus-vodka binge, enduring migraine-inducing debt while Pal demanded a monthly salary despite failing to bring in advertisers, dealing with the stress of having him trap me in my home office so I couldn't leave during his rages, and ultimately having to close the magazine when I failed to convince all of our few advertisers to pay their bills. (There was also a restraining order and a personal move into a 300-square-foot efficiency apartment to recoup and recover, but that's a different book for a different audience.)

While I'm thankful for the opportunity to learn more about magazine publishing from the publisher's point of view, I fully regret the partnership I entered.

While I'm thankful for the opportunity to learn more about magazine publishing from the publisher's point of view, I fully regret the partnership I entered. If I can help someone avoid rushing into a similar mistake, I wish to do so. In chapter eight, we'll look specifically at finding your helpers for any business or industry.

CREATURES OF ENTREPRENEURISM

Entrepreneurism appeals to a specific subset of the workforce. Many of us have ideas and inspirations inside us that don't translate well to logging in at 9:00 a.m. and answering customer service questions all day or punching a proverbial timeclock and handling a retail position. Not everyone is built to always follow another's lead, although there is comfort in knowing someone else has the onus for paying the salaries, benefits, FICA, and so on.

> **There are good dragons of inspiration to pursue and evil monsters that will eat up your energy and reserves.**

How do you know which job you're going to enjoy enough to put in the long hours and sleepless nights for it? The debate of whether a dream *should* require long hours and sleepless nights fits a portion of the book in which we discuss additional responsibilities in our lived reality with time management factored in.

When you know the dream you're working toward is the one that lights up your brain and emotions without fail and is also the one that triggers the desire to stay up late achieving the mini goals that stack to the larger goals, then you're on your way to achieving what you want. You've got the right attitude and motivation to feed your dragon type within. And that's a good thing! Let's move on from that big mistake I made to the positive things we can use for motivation and planning in the real world.

Let's move on to the two species of creatures we're talking about in this book. We'll break those down into four categories later, when we talk about your dragon score in chapter nine. For now, I want you to keep in mind there are good dragons of inspiration to pursue and evil monsters that will eat up your energy and reserves. One of those is great. The other, not so much.

When you have a skill you can nurture and grow to advance your dream, treat it like a powerful fantasy creature that desires your attention as sustenance. Think of it as an internal persuasive helpmate who can help you persevere. Feed that beast and get to the goal.

When you have naysayers and negativity skulking around your dreams, threatening to knock you off track, treat the situation like a demonic monster that

Throw away the distractions and the pessimists who would see you fail.

needs to be eradicated from your life. Throw away the distractions and the pessimists who would see you fail. Focus instead on what you can do to achieve your dreams.

While some of those creatures might require a compromise for life's survival, you'll be able to recognize them and discern which are good — which are the protagonist's helpmates in your hero's journey — after we go through some stories together. Let me be vulnerable for the next chapter and share anecdotes from my life to show you what I mean.

Chapter 2

<u>Lessons from a Kid's Dreams Turned to Realism</u>

When I was in high school, my parents worried about my future. While I wasn't a bad kid, they feared the worst. I was a teenager, after all.

    I had an unhealthy interest in the music on the radio and spent far too much time in my imagination, creating worlds for imaginary characters and creatures to go on epic adventures. Those artistic things were not conducive to selecting a high-value degree at an in-state university that would afford me a comfortable career.

    Thus, my parents discouraged the artistic things.

    One day, my father brought home *What Color is Your Parachute?* by Richard N. Bolles and told me to use it to help find direction for my life. The adult me can recognize lessons and ideas of use in such a book today. Circa 1985, the fifteen-year-old Sandy was horrified by what "a lifetime of meaningful work and career success" truly meant.

I envisioned my parachute as pitch-black, heavy, suffocating canvas with thick, naval-quality ropes tied to anvils a cartoon coyote might throw around. I don't think Mr. Bolles would appreciate me saying this, but at that tender moment in my young life, the book did more to damage my sense of purpose and outlook than my sixth-grade math teacher who'd drawled, "I'm appalled at you," whenever I'd answered a problem incorrectly.

Maybe, the color of the parachute was the wrong question for a creative person who saw symbolism in all things. I envisioned the parachute as an unopening pack strapped to my back as I was shoved out of a plane into an expanse that offered careers in which I had no interest. I didn't want to go into hydroengineering or quantum mechanics or a business call center.

I wanted to write books.

In fact, I'd wanted to write books since I was a small child. I can remember (not fondly; I'm not proud of this) being jealous of a fellow student in fourth grade because our teacher allowed him to read from a spiral notebook in which he wrote

The Muppets fanfiction at night. I was green with envy because I overheard two teachers calling the boy creative and speaking in hushed tones about his genius when I, too, was writing stories.

But I also had an irrational fear that if I stepped up and told my teacher I was writing original stories with characters I'd created in my head, she'd deride me for stealing the boy's spotlight. I'd had a difficult time with a vindictive teacher at a former school during third grade, so my trust issues prevented me from seeing the teachers as likely to support another student being creative.

Luckily, I had a great grandmother and an aunt who saw I was writing stories and enjoying it. They supported and encouraged that passion. And I grew up knowing that's what I wanted to do later in life.

THE DREAM:

Writing books, like the stories I was reading in school, for a career.

For all those reading this book today, let me tell you, there's more than one way to go about making a dream come true. Not every dream is going to be easy to achieve. Not every job is going to be easy to land. Not every promotion is going to be easy to attain. As the cliché tells us, if it were easy, everyone would do it.

THE REALITY:
Writing and editing articles for a career, with book publishing on the side.

You see, as much as it would pain my teenage self to hear the adult Sandy say this, my parents were right. It is not the norm to make a living writing books.

During the 1980s, when my parents were doing everything in their power to discourage my writing habit, we had authors such as J.R.R. Tolkien, David Eddings, Terry Brooks, and Ursula K. Le Guin, who were all the rage for big publishing houses such as Ballantine Books of Random House and Del Rey, Bantam Books, and Futura Publications of Macdonald & Co.

We had not yet conceived the idea of independent publishing houses and print on demand (POD) allowing small presses to manage multiple creatives in short press runs. We had yet to imagine there could be a day when an individual could make a living without the industry doing the business side of it for him or her.

Now, an individual can hire an editor to assist in preparing a manuscript, an artist to create a marketable cover, and a publicist to manage an online campaign. Even with those tools at society's disposal, the market is so glutted with talent (More than 1,300 titles are released per day in North America alone.) it takes a lottery-winning event to get noticed and make a living off that industry."[1,2]

But I'm not writing books to rub elbows with the likes of Stephen King or Margaret Atwood at some swank party of elites or to take the next 64% of the marketplace. I'm writing because it's my dream.

All this to say, my parents were right to push me into finding a career that could allow me to support myself as an adult. I wish their methods had been less demoralizing, but we're all new at something the first time through.

We set our goals and our dreams in the real world. As you can see above, my dream since I was a child has always been to write stories. That's not something I had to give up, but it is something I needed to adjust, making it a side hustle.

Because it's my dream and my passion, it's the extra work I'm willing to put my energy and effort into, during the evenings and on the weekends. We'll talk more about finding the time for our goals in chapter seven, but I want to mention here my dream would have stalled out if I hadn't been willing to compromise and pivot along the way. See how much of the following method, if not this exact play-by-play, you can apply to your ideas.

COLLEGE COMPROMISES
While I don't believe everyone is a good candidate for attending a four-year debt-load institution, I recognize its importance for specific careers. I also recognize the value of a two-year community college and the incredible opportunities trade schools open to wide swaths of our youth. The amount of money to be made from a fulfilling career in a trade is astounding.

The fact of the matter is, the education system in the United States — the one I'm qualified to speak about — prepares us not necessarily to pursue a career, but instead prepares us to continue going to school, thus going further into debt. It is my opinion higher education no longer prepares young adults for reality. Even when my then-fiancé graduated from what was then

Northeast Missouri State University in 1993 with a bachelor's degree in political science, the system hadn't prepared him for a job or a career.*3 It had prepared him to attend another university in New Zealand, to attempt to earn an additional degree.

It's my opinion the K-12 public education system is letting us down. To pick each other up — to pick ourselves up — we must get through the first twelve years of school without succumbing to ennui. We must find a way to excite youth about life beyond a pre-determined four-year institutionalized debt factory.

Please understand me; I believe reading, writing, arithmetic, history, even political science, are important subjects for our youth to learn and understand. Critical thinking needs to be brought back to the masses. I also see the importance of teaching our youth how to support themselves in the real world so they can build up their dreams, and those of their neighbors, in their communities.

> **The amount of money to be made from a fulfilling career in a trade is astounding.**

For me, going to college was almost disastrous. I couldn't afford to go to the huge journalism school in the middle of Missouri where almost every one of my classmates and friends went, yet I wanted to pursue a journalism degree. I had the idea I might go to work for a newspaper like the *New York Times*. Praise God I woke up to the insanity of a daily deadline during my first semester and changed my degree.

Instead, I attended a smaller university in a frigid corner of Missouri where I debated going to class on icy mornings because I was miserably cold. Yes, as ridiculous as it sounds, the weather from 1988 through 1992 nearly derailed my life. Try explaining that to your parents, who are concerned because you're only covered on their insurance as a dependent if you maintain a certain number of class credits per semester. But I made it through Northeast Missouri State University with a degree in English, an emphasis in communications, and a job as a proofreader waiting for me upon my graduation.

STRATEGIC INTERVIEWING
When I was twenty-one years old and preparing to graduate from college with a BA in English, I interviewed at a few companies for positions with magazines and creative productions. One of those was the American Polled Hereford

Association (APHA) in Kansas City. They flew me to their offices for my interview, and Mr. Ed Bible, the editor of the *Polled Hereford Journal*, picked me up at the airport.

I began the interview process with Ed and a woman who handled the production management/artists. They gave me an editing test to mark up while I was seated in his office, and I easily completed that.

The second part of the process was to go into the boardroom where a group of the association's menfolk were ready to get on with their day. I remember one of the gentlemen looking at my resume and snickering as he said, "You have an English degree. Are you planning to write the next great American novel?" He didn't exactly look directly at me as he asked that. And he didn't exactly throw my resume on the boardroom table. It was apparent my degree did not impress him.

I knew what my answer had to be. I laughed politely and said, "Oh, no, no. My focus is going to be on my career."

REAL-WORLD SURVIVAL SKILLS
I worked there for six years, through a few association presidents and a merger with

the American Hereford Association (AHA) downtown. We'll investigate the importance of those changes in the section on perseverance in chapter six. While employed there, I worked on my stories on my own time without anyone needing to know anything about them. My career in magazine publishing and creative marketing materials came first. It paid the bills, including my then-husband's student loans. It covered my health insurance. It kept food in the fridge.

    It wasn't until I went to work for an asphalt paving magazine in 1998 that I started to truly dig the industry and the topic behind my magazine career. Then the career-in-reality that supported the dream I worked on the side started to blend in the enjoyment factor. I was "doing" something I wanted to be doing. My dream and reality became a homogenized mix because I'd done the smart thing by listening to my parents and obtaining a degree — the real-world survival skills — I could use in the real world.

Chapter 3

Conquer the First Few Monsters

Going forward, let's blend discussions of encouragement, faith, mental and physical health and wellness, inspiration, motivation, on-the-job training, and perseverance, which I mentioned in chapter one.

I am a firm believer all boats rise with a rising tide. We are meant to encourage one another and lift one another up. "Be kindly affectioned one to another with brotherly love; in honour, preferring one another; Not slothful in business; fervent in spirit; serving the Lord." (*Authorized King James Version*, 1958, Rom. 12:10-11)

It irks me when I see humans undermine one another, whether that's in business or in society in general. Let me give you a business example you might be able to watch out for in your own career.

Within the example of lifting someone who was a direct-report when I worked at a university in Florida, you'll see several other lessons come into play. One of the first lessons begins in Kansas City, helping someone's mental health and wellness, and encouraging and motivating that person in a new direction.

In the early 2000s, my then-husband was disappointed enough in his job selling advertising at a newspaper he fell into the belief he couldn't do anything else. He allegedly had multiple degrees, and truly was a book-smart fellow, but he felt no one would hire him to do anything other than sell newspaper ads.

A mutual friend and I helped him revamp his resume and did what we could to encourage him to apply for other jobs, but he held firm to a destructive belief. That was not good for his mental health.

He decided he had to go back to school for another degree, but none of the schools in Missouri would suit him. He had his eye on one in Michigan, which I vetoed. (*See the note in chapter two about my inability to function in cold weather.*) I compromised, suggesting, if he had to uproot me from my home, career, church family, and everything I knew, then I would be willing to go to Florida, where I could help with sea turtle conservation.

While I didn't have a degree in biology or an immediate plan for entering a conservation program, I was able to volunteer with a group called Turtle Time once we settled in Southwest Florida. Three sections of Bonita Beach were assigned to me to patrol at first light during sea turtle nesting and hatching months of the year — roughly May through October — and I helped monitor endangered species for almost a decade, only taking time off at doctor's orders during chemotherapy treatments. One of the highlights of my life is rescuing a darling loggerhead hatchling off a basketball court after he'd been disoriented by beachfront lighting.

> **One of the highlights of my life is rescuing a darling loggerhead hatchling off a basketball court after he'd been disoriented by lights.**

The sea turtle success means, yes, my ex-husband found the university from Michigan had moved a segment of its programs into a temporary campus in Florida, he applied, and they accepted him to their graduate program in theology. During our tour of the "campus," the university provost, a kindly priest, turned to me and asked, "What will you do?" When I told him I'd find a job related to magazine publishing, he lit up. He'd been trying to get a community newspaper started. Could I do that?

Yes.

This isn't the place to detail how ill-prepared my future boss was for my arrival, but the provost hired me and handed me over to a person we'll label Dr. C—. She was the director of the development department, which was reported to have had the highest turnover of any in the university. Here's where the idea of *encouraging* our co-workers and colleagues comes in.

Our events director came to my office more than once with tears in his eyes, fearing Dr. C— was going to fire him. I never had the heart to tell him, "No, she has outlined for me the strategy she's using to make your life miserable enough for you to quit." One day J— came to my office with a program he'd paid a vendor to print. On its back page were the words to a hymn to be sung by the congregation at the end of the event. It was also performed in the movie *Sister Act*.

You see where I'm going with this, right?

J— had looked up the song lyrics

with Google, then copied and pasted the words into the layout without noticing which version he'd found. He'd saved the department some money by doing the layout himself.

All two hundred[1] had come back from the printer in time for that night's gathering, and J— was white as a sheet confessing what he'd done, lamenting there was no time to reprint all those programs with the correct words to the hymn, and dreading Dr. C— was going to fire him for sure over it. While he sat in front of my desk popping antacids, I measured the printed area on the back of the program.

I called his assistant in and explained what they needed to do was print the correct lyrics on oversized mailing labels, which she could quickly drive up to OfficeMax to purchase. Then, I would sit down with the two of them, and with all three of us working on it, we could strategically place two-hundred labels on the programs before the evening's event. The three of us were the only ones who needed to know.

His relief was palpable.

Although, in retrospect, he probably would've been happier in the long run if he'd have been fired and freed to seek his "good" dragon. One of my friends who worked there came to tell me she was quitting and was initially angry with me when I told her, "I can't accept your resignation until you have a new job lined up." She later thanked me for preventing her from walking off the job that day.

The point is, those were only two of the people whom I tried to encourage at that institution, and they also encouraged me while I was there.

We start to bloom when we help others grow.

In business, it's important to stop and tell someone they're doing a good job at something. It's kind to use what skills or tools you have at your disposal to lift someone who might be struggling. It's basic common decency to lend a hand when someone is down. We start to bloom when we help others grow, and that makes the work environment beautiful. At least in theory.

I want to apply that concept to the dreams and the goals you might be considering while reading. There are more opportunities to encourage one another than in the workplace. There are more opportunities to share our faith than in the church building on Sunday morning. There are more opportunities to improve our health and wellness than with an annual checkup with a general practitioner. We can be mindful of what inspires and motivates us and share that information with others, when appropriate.

Here's another example that has grown exponentially in the industry where I currently work. Please don't misunderstand what's coming next; I know I'm not the reason Women in Construction (WIC) or Women of Asphalt are successful phenomena. I'm not suggesting that at all here. I'm merely suggesting the spirit of those organizations is something I've understood during my career on the periphery of the asphalt industry.

The construction industry has been dominated by men since its inception. That makes sense, given the physical — and frankly dangerous — nature of the industry since its early days.[*2] When I accepted a position as the associate editor of *Asphalt Contractor* Magazine in 1998, then owned by Group Three Communications in Kansas City, Missouri, you could probably fit the entire number of women working in the asphalt trade in one room.

Within a few months, I'd been promoted to editor of the magazine, and I was firmly ensconced in all things asphalt.

I'd just stepped out of creating materials for the beef cattle industry, so the idea of relating to gruff men working outdoors wasn't a problem. I understood my audience. Each time I learned about a woman being promoted at a public relations or marketing agency, state or national association, contractor or state construction agency, or any other entity, I sent an email congratulating her. I can't recall how many times I started an email with, *"You don't know me, but I believe in supporting women in our industry. I'd like to congratulate and encourage you…"*

Let me tell you something. It takes a huge gulp and a swallowing of my sense of imposter syndrome to send an email like that to a woman who has just been promoted to president and CEO of a multi-million-dollar construction company. It feels somehow patronizing to reach out to a relative stranger who is so much more advanced in her career, so much higher in society than I, and say, *"I'd like to congratulate you and encourage you as a woman in our industry."*

But I swallowed my anxiety each time and did it because, and I cannot stress this enough, it is vital that we encourage one another. That's especially true when we are women in an industry still 85% dominated by men.[*3]

When women in the asphalt industry banded together in 2017 and started an organization called Women of Asphalt, I pounced on the opportunity to highlight women from within and without the group in the pages of *AsphaltPro* every month possible.

While I'd been highlighting women among the executives in the magazine's *Meet the Exec* section, I made the decision to replace the department with *Meet a Woman of Asphalt* with the January 2020 issue. As you might suspect, women aren't quick to rush forward and put themselves in the spotlight. It's like pulling teeth to get a female equipment operator to talk about how she started in the industry. Finding them around North America is more difficult than you'd think.

It is vital that we encourage one another.

Another way I try to encourage, inspire, and motivate others is with the BookTube channel SandySaysRead. That piece of my side hustle is a way for me to showcase other authors while alerting an audience to the fact I exist.

The BookTube concept is one that's been around for well over a decade with social media influencers filming and uploading their book reports. At first blush, that might sound boring, but it's brilliant.

An author friend of mine, who is stellar at encouraging and uplifting others, mentioned BookTube to me during her annual Promo Day event in 2018. Jo Linsdell, whom you can find all around the internet using her name, shared the basics of the phenomenon, explaining all it takes to get started is a built-in web cam and mic, and an internet connection. You basically set up a YouTube channel, call it BookTube, and focus your content creation on books, reading, literature, authors, and the like.

The goal of my BookTube channel is to lift other authors alongside me.

I execute my channel with a focus on indie authors. If an author is published by a small, independent press, I'm going to be more inclined to purchase, read, and review that author's book than one by an author published by one of the "big five" houses with marketing teams and distribution arms behind them. By focusing on those lesser-known names, I've severely limited my channel's popularity, but that's all right.

The mission of SandySaysRead remains the same; to grow an audience that's interested in discovering new authors, new stories, new characters, and so on. My goal is to lift other authors alongside me. Stephen King doesn't need my help with a review on my channel.

Not everyone we encounter in a new job or along the path to realizing our dreams will be interested in encouraging or supporting us. Just because you read this book and internalize the positive vibes doesn't mean your post about the ideas you learn here will be met with positivity on all the social media platforms. As an adult, you understand disappointment in negative humans and keyboard warriors come to life around us. I encourage you to mute and ignore the negative people. "Cast out the scorner, and contention shall go out; Yea, strife and reproach shall cease." (KJV, 1958, Prov. 22:10)

In his best-selling book *Business Relationships That Last*, Ed Wallace — the managing director of AchieveNEXT© Human Capital — points out entire C-suites of corporations struggle with how to leverage or capitalize on the relationship-building we're talking about above.

He terms that relationship-building "relational capital" and reminds us it's fluid in nature. And of course, it is. Business allies will enter and leave your life as you progress toward your ultimate goal(s), and it's up to you to recognize who is receptive to your encouragement, whom you can motivate alongside you, and whom you can count on to reciprocate the assistance on some level (if that's desired/required).

Not everyone we encounter will have the same energy or mindset toward achievement, and that's something we'll discuss more deeply in chapter eight. For now, keep in mind you're setting goals for your dream, not in a void, but among other dreamers and businesspersons who might be excited to work alongside you.

Or they might not.

Build lasting relationships with those people who are working to succeed, but remember the adage some people come into our lives for a reason and some only for a season. As sad as that truism is, sometimes we see relationships break when we are no longer useful to the other person.

Jealous people will try to pull you under because they want to climb higher than you. Visualize a ladder on the side of a swimming pool. If you're on the bottom rung with your head above the water and you're fixin' to go up another rung, the jealous person comes along to pull you back under. The jealous person pulls you off the ladder so he or she might climb up first, higher, faster, or instead of you.

A narcissist will try to pull you under because they see themselves as the one who is worthy of excelling and you as not worthy. You are the bug to be drowned and swirled out of the way. I highly recommend reading Joe Navarro's *Dangerous Personalities* for assessing and handling the potential narcissists in your life if you suspect something nefarious around you. I posted a review of the book on October 3, 2021, on my SandySaysRead channel where you can learn more.

Non-dreamers will try to pull you under, not always purposely, because they can't see the rainbows you see. Let's face it, there are people in our world who are perfectly content to work at a drive-thru window, pick up a six-pack on the way home, and park themselves in front of the television for entertainment after work.

There's nothing wrong with that lifestyle if a person is truly content with it.

We each have a different level of energy or desire when it comes to striving or struggling for something beyond a job in a cubicle. But beware of how a non-motivated person might be affecting your attitude toward your goals if that person also consistently guilts you into sitting in front of the television with the six-pack.

That person doesn't necessarily understand your goals and dreams are important to you. As harsh as it sounds, that person might be a hindrance. You might need to spend less time around the person.

The people you spend time with influence your energy as well as your actions. As former U.S. Secret Service agent and current multi-media journalist Evy Poumpouras teaches us in her book, *Becoming Bulletproof,* your circle matters. The inner circle of people in your business and your personal life can be a help or a hindrance to you and to accomplishing your mission. Curate that circle, as we'll discuss in

Miracles start to happen when you give as much energy to your dreams as you give to your fears, Energize the dragons and see what great things start to happen!

chapter eight, so you have positive, inspirational, helpful, and hopeful people around you. The use of an inner circle will come up again in chapter nine when we determine how well you fit into the shoulder dragon category.

So far, I've offered examples of chasing dreams mostly from my own experience. Let's devote the next chapter to a gentleman from the asphalt industry who provides an example of achieving a dream while employed fulltime. Alan Jeffrey (A.J.) Ronyak is the proprietor of Asphalt Solutions, Inc., now headquartered in Florida, and he offers a great lesson in encouragement, inspiration, and perseverance. He exemplifies the entrepreneur who achieved a dream "on the side."

Chapter 4

A.J. Takes on an Asphalt Monster

In 1996, the owner of Thompson-McCully Co. in Michigan, Bob Thompson, sought out A.J. to come work for him at his Rawsonville, Michigan division. A.J. had built an asphalt plant from the ground up for a company on the far side of Detroit, and that attracted Bob's attention.

A.J. instituted some repairs, to the tune of $278,000, at the Rawsonville plant for Bob and proved himself a smart hire. He said he was the plant manager of what was touted as the first "world's largest asphalt plant."

"It was the 'superplant'," A.J. said. "It was rated 750 tons per hour, but there were times I had it going up to 1,000 tons an hour. In my last season there, from April 18 to November 22, I produced 998,000 tons of hot-mix asphalt. That broke every company record. Part of the plant was a Dillman plant. I ran dual fuels on it and was cleaning the filters all the time. I had a really good ground guy."

A.J. knew what he was doing and how to keep an asphalt plant in shape. He also knew he had a problem to solve when nearby community members complained about asphalt odors.

"I was spraying [an odor masking agent popular at the time] in the stack to mitigate the smell, but it wasn't working," A.J. explained. He modified a specialized nozzle to atomize the liquid product that was intended to solve the odor problem, but it still didn't reduce the scent of industry drifting toward the neighborhood on windy days or nights.

One day, while considering the problem, A.J. took out a pack of gum and had his "aha!" moment. Why couldn't he take the oils that make gum smell so good and inject something similar into the liquid asphalt cement (AC) to make it smell good? Or to eliminate the asphalt smell altogether?

He started to experiment on his own time. "I had shipping containers for

> **Notice throughout A.J.'s story, he's mentioning the people around him. He gives props to the people who were integral to success at the day job and the side hustle. That's an attitude of gratitude we don't want to miss!**

our workshops in the yard and I started monkeying around in one of those for a workstation. I would heat up small samples of AC. I was using eye droppers and spearmint oil."

The spearmint oil concept wasn't as far-fetched as one might think. Here's where the concepts of partnering, encouragement, and relational capital sneak in; A.J. contacted the Wrigley family. The gum people. "I actually know the Wrigley family. They turned me on to my current manufacturer in Chicago."

During the experimenting phase, A.J. worked a demanding full-time job. Anyone who's worked in construction knows there are times of the year when you're going full tilt. For Thompson-McCully, there were stretches when the plant A.J. managed ran twenty-four hours a day. He worked fifteen to seventeen of those hours, drove seventy-five minutes to get home, got about four hours of sleep, and drove seventy-five minutes back to do it all again.

Catching time to work on chemical experiments wasn't easy. But A.J.'s good dragon, the goal he was fixed on, was to devise a product that would solve a problem not only for his boss, but also for the asphalt industry at large.

"You've gotta come up with a solution if you've got a problem sitting in front of you."

That's what he did.

He currently holds patents in the United States, Canada, and Europe for his asphalt solutions products.[1] Those are products that suppress components that cause the odor in the liquid AC used in asphalt pavement mixes and asphalt roofing mixes. In 2004, he won the NOVA award from the Construction Innovation Forum (CIF) for his AS Cherry fume-free HMA product.[2]

He has international distributors, customers, and partners. His solution is a resounding success and a benefit to communities not only because it eliminates odors but also because it reduces greenhouse gas emissions. A.J. was ahead of his time when it comes to aiding the asphalt industry on its road to net zero. He even modified the concept to produce AG-ODOR Orange Juice, which is a cold-press, custom-blended additive that virtually eliminates offensive odors in a wide variety of agricultural applications.

He did all of that work without a degree in chemistry and began it without leaving his full-time job, all because he had the desire to do it. He worked hard and with the resources he had.

Those resources included people.

We already mentioned the Wrigley family, who assisted with information and connections. When A.J. showed Bob Thompson what the asphalt odor suppressant he'd created could do all those years ago, the company owner couldn't believe his nose, and immediately contacted the National Center for Asphalt Technology (NCAT) at Auburn University on A.J.'s behalf. As of press time, Auburn University is awarding its first honorary alumni status through the Samuel Ginn College of Engineering to A.J. for his innovations and continuing partnership with NCAT.[3]

When Bob was ready to retire, he sold the asphalt business, which boasted ten asphalt plants, and shared the proceeds with his employees. A.J. took his windfall and invested it in his new venture, starting a company that manufactured and sold an additive that was a game-changer for the elimination of odors at asphalt plants.

A.J. wasn't alone as he worked all those long hours. His wife, Patricia, helped keep life on an even keel.

"Patty was working for Northwest

Airlines, so we were working different shifts. I'd get off my shift, work on the odor suppressant after the second shift came in, drive home, grill up some food, get a few hours of sleep, and start it all over again." He and Patty met each other coming and going, but they kept life together that way.

"It wasn't easy, but I did it. You've gotta have the heart for it, I guess. You've gotta have a reason. Then try not to give up. Sometimes you get let down on occasion. But if there's a will, there's a way."

A.J.'s schedule from the late nineties sounds a little hectic.

He said, "In the peak, at my plant, toward the latter years, we were running twenty-four hours a day. I ran and managed the plant, took care of all the deliveries of materials — rock, AC, additives — ordering parts and maintenance. I'd work fifteen to seventeen hours a day. Sometimes I'd work on the odor suppressant on the weekends or after the second shift came in

BE A DRAGON:

Find time.

Make time.

You can do it!

because I found the time. I made the time for it. We had a company charge at the Holiday Inn just down the road so sometimes I'd just sleep at the Holiday Inn for a few hours so I could head to the plant in the middle of the night."

It sounds like a grueling schedule, and it's not one every entrepreneur is cut out for. As our next entrepreneur, Bryce Wuori of Pavewise in Bismarck, North Dakota will share with us in chapter five, we can end up running ourselves into the ground when we're chasing our dreams if we're not careful.

In A.J.'s case, working in Michigan, the paving season is just that — seasonal. The contractors there must make hay while the sun shines, so the work is consolidated into a short number of months, typically April through October or November. While that means A.J.'s long hours were exhausting and kept him and Patty passing each other like the Dunkin Donuts man from those '70s commercials, those hours weren't "forever."

There was a light at the end of the tunnel. A.J.'s drive to solve the asphalt industry's odor problem kept him focused and he made it to the goal. Now let's take a look at Bryce's story and learn some of the tips he suggests for working a side hustle without burning out.

Chapter 5

Bryce Fixes All the Monsters

Bryce Wuori is the proprietor of Pavewise LLC headquartered in Bismarck, North Dakota. His amazing wife, Brittany, is the COO for the company. She handles marketing and keeping Bryce from overloading himself. Throughout this chapter where we look at the importance of the side hustle in Bryce's work life, take note of the way he's shifted perspective and gives credit to Brittany for helping him recognize when he needs downtime.

As A.J.'s story highlighted in the last chapter, there's a seasonality to the construction industry. Companies in construction must pack much of their productivity into the times of the year when weather allows perishable material workability and cure time.

That means workers can be pushed to the limit working overtime in between weather events. Bryce has developed a cloud-based software app that helps companies navigate project schedules, as well as employee mental health status and progress during projects for everyone's most productive, healthiest, quality results. The software has his company's name, Pavewise, but came about while he was working fulltime for Geophysical Survey Systems, Inc., of Nashua, New Hampshire and consulting for asphalt contractors. The groundbreaking innovation was his dream on the side.

And it wasn't his first.

"I've been side-hustling my whole life," Bryce told me. "Not because I had to but because I always wanted to. If something can be performed more efficiently, I'm gonna build it."

Bryce started out as a full-time asphalt engineer for Northern Improvement Company, headquartered in Fargo, North Dakota, when he noticed a smaller dirt-working company leaving a void in the marketplace. He saw the need for dirt work in the region, approached his boss about starting a side business to do the work, and began the project with less overhead and more efficiency.

> "I've been side-hustling my whole life. Not because I had to but because I wanted to." —Bryce Wuori

When that became more successful than he originally thought it would, Bryce moved on to the next full-time job with a side hustle in asphalt consulting. That, too, started to grow beyond its original intent, and Bryce was developing the side project with Pavewise to solve problems for clients.

With each change, he's remained on good terms with former bosses, keeping good relationships in place and "smart people" around him.

"I surrounded myself with people smarter than me and I learned from them. My dad and the quality engineer at Northern, for example. And I always left those jobs in good standing," he stressed.

"There's always full transparency, which is important. Some companies want the worker's full attention, so it's not as easy to work on a side hustle. Since COVID, people have needed that something extra to do.

"Now I'm running a software company with nine employees. Each company has started as a side hustle that grew. I worked my regular job during regular hours, but I'm typically up at 4:30 or 5:00 in the morning doing my 'non-job' and doing it on the weekends."

That loaded schedule is something we saw in A.J.'s story, and while it's often necessary for the entrepreneur who's working a day job to survive while building the dream project, it's also easy for the entrepreneur to experience an overload. Bryce offered his story as a cautionary tale against letting yourself get spread too thin.

Because he worked a demanding full-time job while assisting with caring for a growing young family while developing a side hustle he was passionate about, he found himself saying "yes" to every opportunity he possibly could in an effort to keep momentum going. That led to physical and mental burnout.

"Early in my career, I didn't balance work and life and side hustle, and that's why I got to the point where I had a mental breakdown. There were times when my wife had to remind me to eat. She knew that and did a lot to take care of me. All of our kids were quite a bit younger, so I tried to do as much work as I could when everyone else was sleeping — before everyone else was up. I didn't take lunch breaks.

> **He found himself saying "yes" to every opportunity he possibly could in an effort to keep momentum going.**

"Now I've turned over a new leaf. Now when I get up in the mornings, I read a book I want to read, or I meditate, or I stretch. I used to love reading and I'd gotten away from it. Little things like that go a long way.

"A lot of highly driven people do go through that burnout because you don't know your limit until you hit it. It's a learning process. Pushing those limits."

Bryce shared he entered a cycle of overworking and trying to remain caffeinated to stay awake, which affected his health and his outlook.

"I learned what can I handle as a person. I now know thresholds — I know when I need to take a break because of how I'm sleeping or eating.

"Brittany was a PRN at the hospital for some of that time and worked out of the home some of that time. We tag-teamed caring for the kids as business partners and life partners. She notices when I need to de-stress — she knows how I function."

Having Brittany as a partner is key to Bryce's mental health. He also offers ideas he's internalized since his mental health epiphany — ideas that have helped him in business:

FIRST: GET SOMEBODY ELSE'S OPINION.
When you ask for someone else's thoughts, it distributes the evaluation of an opportunity among the team members; different perspectives come in.

SECOND: GIVE A DECISION A LITTLE TIME TO MARINATE.
When you have a decision to make, or an opportunity to take or pass on, give yourself time to make the decision. Let it be a natural progression instead of forced and you might find the opportunity isn't all it's cracked up to be.

"Knowing when to say 'no' is important, too," Bryce shared. "I tend to see opportunities as 'this could be my next big ticket' until I give them some time and think them through more carefully."

Bryce's logical approach to considering opportunities thoughtfully and with a partner or team resonates with the idea of slowing down. Not everything has to be accomplished overnight.

Often, the excitement of identifying a dream or seeing that fancy dragon we want to capture gets us in a state that makes it easy to overload and overwork. It takes a great deal of discipline to follow Bryce's advice. Change might be coming at a new entrepreneur quickly, but taking the race slowly and steadily could be the key to winning. We'll look at perseverance amid change in the next chapter as we start diving into some exercises. If you haven't already been making notes in the margins, it's time to grab a pen!

HEALTHY DRAGONS FROM BRYCE'S STORY:

- Know your limits
- Remember to eat healthfully
- Know how to de-stress healthfully
- Seek input from others, preferably your team
- Don't make big decisions too quickly; think through "opportunities" carefully
- It's okay to say "no" to some opportunities
- Your dream doesn't have to happen overnight—and probably won't. Don't be in a rush!

PART TWO:
Let's Start Building

Chapter 6

Embrace the Dragon of Change

We need to give some attention to the topic of perseverance. Change doesn't have to be a bad thing; we don't have to view it as a monster, but as one of those good dragons to go after. The examples I can share with authority are my own, so let's dive in.

  We'll start with high school marching band, which not only taught me the importance of working with a team, as both A.J.'s and Bryce's examples reinforced, but also taught me endurance. We marched around in the heat and humidity of July and August in St. Louis to prepare for the schoolyear and upcoming football and contest season

> **Reach down inside and pull a little more out.**

where we'd be performing. The high school band teacher, Mr. Ron Curtis, would use a bullhorn to shout commands across the crisp brown grass of the practice field.

To this day, I repeat to myself his refrains of, "No guts, no glory" and, "No pain, no gain" when I find myself slacking or slowing down. I remember him telling us, "Band, I know you're tired. Reach down inside and pull a little more out. You can do this."

Somehow, there's a reserve inside every one of us for the things we consider important. Inside all of us, there's a well from which we pull the sustenance to keep grinding on toward our dreams. When I feel tired, when I feel defeated by someone who's answered, "No" to a marketing opportunity or an online troll who's said, "You totally suck," I remember Mr. Curtis telling us, "No guts, no glory." I move on to the next task.

> **For Stephen, the good dragon he nurtures is resilience.**

More recently, my new *Choices* Series publisher, Stephen Zimmer of Seventh Star Press, ended one of our phone calls saying, "Stay relentless." He's got the right attitude. He has the dragon of persistence in his soul.

Stephen's day job intertwines with his dream. As the publisher and an editor at Seventh Star Press, he's able to work within the industry he loves.

"The dream is storytelling," he shared. "I'm working in the sphere of storytelling, whether that's editing, publishing, or working on the Imaginarium Convention. I like the fact it's all connected, but right now I must provide more services in the industry to make a living."

For Stephen, the good dragon he nurtures is resilience. "My dragon is the one that stays relentless. No matter how depressing things might get around you, the survivor with an eye toward moving forward — I would describe my dragon in that form."

Both Stephen and I have had careers in publishing that have seen changes in the industry and watching those changes has required "sticktoitiveness." Let me give you as quick of a summary as I can so you understand where I'm coming from.

I've already shared with you I worked at a cattle publication for six years upon graduating college. The perseverance there was rolling with the punches through a hiring and a wage freeze, the removal of the association president, a merger with another association and move to that entity's headquarters in downtown Kansas City, and seeing my first boss, Ed Bible, resign."[1]

When Ed left the association, his suggestion that a few of us follow his example didn't fall on deaf ears. I interviewed with a construction magazine group in 1998 and learned the importance of flexibility. When I arrived at Group Three Communications, the married couple who hired me didn't know which publication they'd assign me to until the day I walked in. It would either be the crane or the asphalt magazine.

I'm thankful they chose asphalt.

The perseverance through changes at that post involved Group Three Communications splitting in half with *Asphalt Contractor* and *Bridge Builder* magazines moving to another company and location. I'm not sure I remember the name we were under, but I remember the gentleman who owned it, Bill Neeley, being a fireball of energy and ideas. He was an older gentleman who embodied the definition of an entrepreneur. He would pull a chair up to my desk in my office and announce, "Lady, I've got an idea!"

That could've been awesome, or it could've been something to gently dissuade and redirect. Either way, it was going to be interesting.

After a couple of years, Bill's company sold to a fledgling, investor-based publishing group called Mercor Media, which also bought the other magazines that had originally belonged to Group Three. The family was back together again, but changes kept coming with three presidents in a short timeframe before Mercor Media needed to sell *Asphalt Contractor* to make some loan payments.

I learned which corporate entity they were going to sell my publication to and went on a quick job hunt. My perseverance with head-office alterations had come to an end, but having stayed through the corporate politics and different presidential styles gave me a skill set for navigating all manner of career changes.

Perseverance has been necessary in the side hustle, as well. I'm sure you don't need me to explain the concept of "it's difficult to get published." The story for my epic fantasy series began circa 1985, when I was daydreaming in chemistry class and saw my main character, Amanda Chariss. I worked on her adventures sporadically for over a decade before I had the tale ready to edit into something I considered shoppable.

Once I'd completed the manuscript for *Choices Meant for Gods*, which exceeded two hundred thousand words, I needed to find an agent to represent the work. That was during the early 2000s, when querying an agent involved putting a letter, printed on resume paper, into an envelope with a self-addressed, stamped return envelope for the agent's assistant's convenience in sending back a slip of paper known as a form rejection.

I researched the top few agents who were accepting fantasy fiction manuscripts (I recall there being fewer than ten at the time.) and selected the top three I wanted to work with. I won't spell out the name of the one who was my absolute number one favorite, but everything about her bio in *The Writers Guide* resonated with me. She requested the first three chapters, but ultimately sent a pleasant rejection, which included the phrasing, "I couldn't get excited about the book."

After wallowing in self-pity and a highball of amaretto for an evening, I got myself together and revised the manuscript. I took her words to heart and fixed the thing. I made it something an agent *could* get excited about. Of course, I also sold my house and moved halfway across the continent during that time, so the agent-and-editor search was essentially on hold for a couple of years.

When I was ready to shop the manuscript again in 2005, I went directly to a publisher at the indie publishing house ArcheBooks Publishing, then of Cape Coral, Florida. We sat down at a writers' conference in Naples, and I pitched Bob Gelinas the story. He asked to read it. A couple of weeks later, Bob sent me a contract. Success!

Fast forward to 2019. After ArcheBooks moved into a new state, and corporate changes mixed with other factors, the company closed its doors. My trilogy went out of print. Luckily, my rights reverted to me, so I shopped my series again.

That time, Seventh Star Press of Lexington, Kentucky took up the trilogy to release all three books simultaneously with revisions, additional scenes, new covers, and new life. My foundational series was remastered and back in print June 2023. By December 2023, I could announce *Choices Meant for Gods* had won a Notable Indie award from Shelf Unbound Media.

Now, other books of mine have won various accolades. I've won awards for my technical writing as an editor, but to have that first, foundational work finally recognized was thrilling. I'll admit right here I was emotional when I opened the congratulatory note.

That's perseverance paying off.

**"CHANGE IS ABOUT THE NARROWEST AND HARDEST GROOVE A MAN CAN GET IN."
—G.K. Chesterton**

There's a saying the only thing that doesn't change is change itself. If you're seeking a job today, rest assured, some strange new technology a year or five from now will throw a wrench in that job's inner workings and you'll need to expand your skills or knowledge to stay current. That's not a hardship if you stay abreast of changes as they come along, if you read and internalize Spencer Johnson's *Who Moved My Cheese?*.

Take it from a magazine editor who has used an X-ACTO knife to cut clip art to paste into a layout on a light table. Now, I create quick banner ads in Canva and place those online. I can remember standing beside the processor in the dark room, waiting for black and white cattle images to develop so I could tag them for the printer to place them in layouts. Now, I upload digital images to a cloud.

All that to say, one way to persevere in either a career or the pursuit of a side hustle is to roll with the punches. Learn new skills as necessary and grow with the company of which you're a part. Don't be afraid of changes, but know the boundaries you're not willing to go beyond.

Now, yes, it's frightening to step out of a job to which you've grown accustomed. When the asphalt publication for which I worked from 1998 to 2003 was being sold (a second time) to help Mercor Media pay its debts, I didn't want to leave the asphalt industry periphery.

I enjoyed writing about and editing articles in that sector of construction. I had friends and colleagues I was going to miss, some of whom I remained in contact with after I went to Uhlig Communications in Kansas. It was scary to step out of my comfort zone and

> **Don't be afraid of changes, but know the boundaries you're not willing to go beyond.**

the familiar pattern of monthly deadlines in an industry I'd learned so much about, but I wasn't going to subject myself to what I knew of the entity the publication was being sold to. I set my boundary and stuck to it.

You might be feeling a sense of worry for the future. Maybe the idea of starting a career or changing jobs is weighing on you and that's why you have this book in your hands. I will tell you, I've had those moments in my career more often than I can count. I will also tell you there is incredible peace in remembering God has our future in His hands. "For I know the thoughts that I think toward you, saith the Lord, thoughts of peace, and not of evil, to give you an expected end." (KJV, 1958, Jer. 29:11)

Several translations, including the *Good News Bible* I learned from as a child, use phrasing of, "I know the plans I have for you" and, "plans for prosperity and not disaster" in that verse. The spirit of the verse is God has a plan for each of us that doesn't involve destruction and despair. We don't have to be fearful of the future.

During one of those moments when I felt the weight of changes in publishing, I was praying and asking, "What am I going to do if this falls apart?" An incredible peace washed over me as a reminder seeped into my mind, as if God was saying, "Child, I hold your future; you have no need to fear."

I felt the pressure lift from my chest and shoulders with those words in my brain and I want you to feel that same lightness and surety. I want you to remember there are at least 3,573 promises of God in the Bible (Source: BibleInfo.com), but I recall an old Southern Baptist preacher in Citrus County, Florida telling the congregation a much higher number than that. I wish now that I'd written it down when he said it because it's a comforting reminder our Creator offers us a secure future in Him. We need only pause and remember to feel the peace of it.

> **We don't have to be fearful of the future.**

We need only persevere in our job search, in our goal setting, in our pursuit of a dream. As I'll discuss in chapter eleven, there might come a point where you pivot and change the goal, but there's no need to fear the outcome. As changes come at you, perseverance and endurance win the day.

Chapter 7

Exercises for Dreaming Your Career into Being

I promise not to ask the color of your parachute, but I *am* going to ask you to stop and consider the thing you're passionate about. I'm going to ask you to grab a pen and write down the first one (or two) topics that excite you in the space right here:

    Do you want to help save an endangered species? Do you enjoy sculpting shrubberies? Do you have a flair for decorating mini cupcakes and tiny cookies? Do you want to work on the international space station? Do you have ideas for curing a rare disease a dear friend from your childhood suffered?

One way to approach your desire is to look at your current skill set.

Think about that for a few minutes. I encourage you to pray about the skills you believe you've been blessed with, to discern what God might be placing in front of you. We've been taught: "Trust in the Lord with all your heart and lean not on your own understanding; in all your ways submit to Him, and He will make your paths straight." (KJV, 1958, Prov. 3:5-6)

Consider it all and use the facing page to write down:

"What skills do I currently possess that I can link to my ultimate business goals?"

As you start listing your skills, you'll probably think of more than what will fit on the page. That's great! Use the margins over here on this side of the spread to write more. Grab scratch paper to write more. Don't let the page limit you!

MY SKILLS ASSESSMENT LIST:

Your next question needs not a list, but an essay for an answer. Again, don't let this empty page limit you. Grab some scratch paper if you need it to answer this question:

"How can I use the skills listed on the last page to start building my business or my side hustle?"

MY BUSINESS PLANNING PARAGRAPH:

Going from a skills list to thoughts of a business plan skips a number of steps in between, but I want you to connect what you're capable of (reality) with the dream job or dream career down the line. I hope the short exercise forced you to consider what your end goal truly requires of you.

For example, if you want to start a lawn care service that shapes and sculpts the landscaping features in upscale communities, do you have the basic strength to lift and wield the tools necessary for the job? Are you allergic to fresh-cut grass? If all you need is an allergy medication and a trailer to haul your equipment, your skills assessment list and business planning paragraph help you figure that out.

> **Connect what you're capable of (reality) with the dream.**

Depending on your comfort level with the rise of the AI machines, you might be willing to type some prompts into one of the myriad AI tools available to you to assess your business idea. It's certainly easier and faster to perform market analysis today than it was when I gathered data on potential competitors to my companion parrot magazine in 2012.

I'm not going to recommend one specific AI tool for performing market research, but I will caution against using the large language models (LLMs) for such a refined project. Something like ChatGPT, Bard, or HuggingChat will be broad — for lack of a kinder term — in its functionality and prone to returning "misinformed" results.

When performing market analysis, you want to discover and uncover potential competitors' websites, blogs, social media and YouTube channels, and the like. You want to gather specific ideas of what works and what doesn't while you're in research mode, but also take notes for what you'll need to build online. You might decide to use AI tools to do the heavy lifting — the laborious parts.

For example, if you dig up three research papers of ninety pages each, you can feed those documents to an AI tool like Afforai, or to a lesser extent, Consensus, and let it summarize the text for you.

Is that cheating? Do I personally find it unsettling to skip educating yourself fully on your competition and marketplace? Yes. But I also see the wisdom in making your research process easier and faster.

Another action you'll want to take is that of analyzing your potential customer. You can call that person your "audience," as well.

The product or service you're building must resonate with your audience; you must be able to speak to your audience with your story (your why), as we discussed in chapter two; you must be able to solve that person's pain point. This means you want to know your potential customer inside and out.

You could also let an AI tool like Qwary scour the internet for surveys of your target audience — to then feed you the results of those surveys — and for conversations in forums and/or social media platforms where your target audience congregates online (which something like GummySearch can help with).

The point is to let an AI tool do the laborious work of market analysis for you.

Not every business will require a blog to communicate with potential customers; some businesses can get away with a blog instead of a website; some businesses use web pages only built off social media platforms or podcast / vlogging hosting services.

While that's one way to let another entity do the heavy lifting of building a framework for your site or your information, it's also one way to lose everything if that entity is purchased by a bad actor or files bankruptcy. As my parrot magazine web designer once cautioned me, "Don't build your house on rented land."

The analysis I've suggested above can help you determine the viability of your dream. As I've been trying to keep

---

SOME AI TOOLS THAT ARE SPECIFIC TO MARKET ANALYSIS

Name	Basic Use
Afforai	summarizes docs
Appen	data training
Browse AI	website scraper
Coefficient	imports data
Consensus	summarizes data
Crayon	reviews competition
Current AI	tracks trends
Kimola	summarizes reviews
Quantilope	auto-researching
Qwary	summarizes surveys
Remesh	focus group tool
SurveyMonkey Genius	conducts/evaluates surveys
YouScan	analyzes social media

Please recognize the second column in this chart offers an oversimplified "summary" of what each tool performs, but this gives a general starting point for your understanding.

at the forefront of our discussion, we are in the real world. Real businesses crash and burn every day, so you want to set your sights on a goal that can not only be achieved but can also be maintained. Let's look at what you're assessing.

MARKET ANALYSIS: For our lawn care example, a potential businessperson might look at the potential for high-end lawn care needs, golf course care needs, or sports facilities care needs versus residential property manager needs, commercial property needs, and so on. The entrepreneur will get a realistic picture of where there's a void in the local marketplace and what he or she might bring to it.

That's what you want to do with your idea or dream — figure out where in the market your service will fit. What solution does your dream offer for others, or is it needed at all?

COMPETITOR ANALYSIS: No matter what business idea you have, look at the companies already serving the market.

Assess such things as their pricing structure, market position, branding and messaging, corporate structure, available inventory, and so on. Not only can you learn from what they're doing right — and wrong — but you can see how best to leverage your strengths, weaknesses, opportunities, and threats (SWOT), which is the next step.

SWOT COMPARISON: Analyze your strengths, weaknesses, opportunities, and threats. Then, compare your product or company, based on SWOT, with the competitors in the marketplace."[1]

 Let me admit to you right here, yes, it's easy for me to see my weaknesses and wallow in self-doubt. Please push past that if you're noticing your weaknesses more easily than your strengths.

 While it's wise to analyze a weakness and find a way to overcome it or place supports around it, you don't want that negative voice of derision to overpower you. Please don't let this step's two "negative" facets derail what could be fantastic and amazing growth. Instead, let's take a deeper dive into how this step works in your favor.

 When analyzing your **strengths**, think about skills you already have and those you're working on. Think about assets or finances you have for your upcoming business. How about your reputation in your community; are you already a known figure? Have you already received some awards or recognition? In the lawn care example, the entrepreneur might already have a fantastic landscaper who's willing to join the team. That's a great strength.

Use this space to write down three of your greatest strengths and how you can leverage each one:

Strength 1:
A way to leverage strength 1:

Strength 2:
A way to leverage strength 2:

Strength 3:
A way to leverage strength 3:

When analyzing your **weaknesses**, don't let a skill shortage get you down. You want to take note of it because that's something you'll work on, but the only way to know what to work on is to identify it. We have an adage in the construction industry that you cannot manage what you don't measure. So let's measure.

Maybe you have someone on your team who is fresh out of school and short on experience. That's not a problem but it can be a weakness in the marketplace. Make a note of it so you have identified where you need training or growth.

Use this space to write down three of your greatest weaknesses and how you will improve each one:

Weakness 1:
A way to improve weakness 1:
Weakness 2:
A way to improve weakness 2:
Weakness 3:
A way to improve weakness 3:

When analyzing your **opportunities**, look outside yourself and your immediate team. This is the moment to look for partnerships, alliances, and outside assistance. Are there grants or other types of funding you could apply for? Are there training services you could take advantage of to help your team members or yourself? Is there a project in your community that needs your set of skills to come to fruition that will become your launching point?

Use this space to write down three of your greatest opportunities and how you can capitalize on each one:

Opportunity 1:
A way to capitalize on opportunity 1:

Opportunity 2:
A way to capitalize on opportunity 2:

Opportunity 3:
A way to capitalize on opportunity 3:

When analyzing your **threats**, look inward and outward. Look at your negative thoughts that can be reformed and look to the marketplace where competitors might be circling like vultures. While you don't want to start your venture from a place of fear, you don't want to be blindsided by a competitor's ability to sweep an opportunity out from under you or by a change in the marketplace.

You've identified opportunities in the last exercise. Don't lose those because you overlook a threat such as competition, financial burdens, negative team members, supply chain disruption, or some other issue you could resolve if you see it now.

Certainly, use the margins on these pages to write in extra information if you need to. Make the most of this whole SWOT exercise and identify extra strengths or extra tactics for leveraging the "points" you identify as those thoughts reveal themselves to you. And use the space reserved on the facing page to write down three of your greatest threats and how you will overcome and master each one:

Threat 1:
A way to thwart threat 1:
Threat 2:
A way to thwart threat 2:
Threat 3:
A way to thwart threat 3:

ACTIONABLE STEPS: Let's delve deeply into your actionable steps. They'll differ depending on where you are on the road to your end goal.

If you're looking for a first job, seeking a different job, or building the side hustle, the actionable steps might be the mini goals you need to set to start a business, to move up in your career, to expand a current business, and so on. Set these goals accordingly, based on the analyses above.

In chapter one, we mentioned staying up late to achieve the mini goals that stack up to the larger ones. I recognized the idea of stackable goals in Chelsea A. Ellis' *Fail to Success*. She described the concept as accomplishing goals in chunks, which makes perfect sense. By accomplishing a small goal that leads to the next small goal that leads to the next small goal, you can accomplish chunks of goals toward the larger, main goal.

> **You don't have to do everything all at once. You stack your goals so one mini-goal leads to another.**

What I want you to do for this next exercise, for stacking your goals, is another tactile one. Write the main goal you've thought of while reading through this book at the top of the next spread (page 106). Beneath it, write down something you must do to reach that goal.

For example, if you want to get a contract to maintain the grounds at the local golf resort, the goal beneath that might be to present a four-color portfolio of your work — with a QR code linking to your website of testimonials — to the manager of the resort.

Beneath that, write down something you must do to reach that goal. For our "golf resort presentation" example, you would need to print a brochure to take to your meeting.

All the way down the next page, write in things that need to be accomplished to help reach the main goal at the top. (E.g.: Build a website. Get testimonials. Buy lawn care equipment. Book the meeting with the manager.)

Don't worry if the mini goals you think of get out of order as you write. You can number them later if you wish. The point is to make your brain think through how to achieve the goal. Scatter and splatter the ideas onto the page as they come to you.

Then, let your brain (and central nervous system) recognize you don't have to do it all at once. You can hit those mini goals to stack your way to the prize.

WRITE YOUR MAIN GOAL HERE:

┌─────────────────────────────────────┐
│   │
│   │
└─────────────────────────────────────┘

WRITE ADDITIONAL, ACTIONABLE GOALS TO STACK:

IMPLEMENT THE PLAN: When you've assigned the actionable steps to yourself or members of your inner circle or team, it's time to grow!

I recognize many actionable steps these days include marketing. Even the made-up example of expanding a lawn care business had a promotional brochure and a website in it. I want to take that concept into social media influencing territory for a moment.

Not everyone is cut out to be a social media influencer on YouTube. But I've started to believe having a YouTube channel is the 2020s' version of having a website. According to Think Media, 64% of participants in a national poll said they watch YouTube more than they watch television. "The eyeballs are on YouTube — you just need to get in front of them."

Think Media also shared from what they called "the largest nationwide study of content creators," 42% of the participants in the study were more likely to work with a service provider

> **"64% of participants in a national poll said they watch YouTube more than they watch television."**
> **— Think Media**

if said provider had a YouTube channel. In other words, real estate agents, coaches, personal trainers, dieticians, people who offer a service are advised to be on YouTube for that extra boost in credibility.

As with the building of a website, building a YouTube presence takes finesse. There are, as luck would have it, videos about how to do it.

You can take free or paid courses online or at the local library about how to get started. When I was ready to start my BookTube channel in 2018, you can bet I studied DIY videos about setting up microphones, web cameras, and lighting; how to set up the channel itself; backdrops and depth of field; theme and software for both filming and editing. The list goes on and on. Because the YouTube channel is secondary to my book publishing business, which is the side hustle I love, I didn't do anything as crazy as quitting the day job and investing all the time necessary to create and build a full-time "influencer" channel.

That's not my why.

Building a channel on a platform such as YouTube, Rumble, X (formerly Twitter), or any other gives you instant access to the wide audience already using those sites. YouTube is still the second highest used search engine after Google. But YouTube plays by its own rules, which it is free to alter whenever and however it chooses.

If you monetize a channel there to sell your virtual widgets to an audience you build over twelve to fourteen months, that will be a year of wasted time and energy if the algorithm changes drastically and your content is no longer of value or allowed by the censors.

Instead, you might be building a business that requires a satellite office, a garage for equipment, or a boutique for customers to visit. That won't necessarily rely on Rumble or Instagram feeding videos to an audience on a reliable basis.

A whole new set of complications comes with a physical location instead. Now the concept of safety takes on more importance. I'm not going to pretend to be a safety manager, but I'll give you at least a starting point for remembering its importance.

THE 5S HOUSEKEEPING SAFETY CONCEPT
With this safety program, you're basically creating a clean and a safe environment while taking stock of what you have on hand. This program gives you the opportunity to not only improve the safety

of your operations, but also to inventory and assess your needs.

S – Sort through your equipment, materials, ingredients, inventory, etc.

S – Straighten up the shop, office, work truck, food truck/kitchen, and so on.

S – Shine it up by cleaning, sanitizing, removing dangerous grease or hazardous chemicals, etc.

S – Standardize how product inventory, equipment, supplies, and the like are categorized, brought in, re-ordered, and so on.

S – Sustain your new housekeeping program, which takes self-discipline. By maintaining the new program, you're keeping tools, supplies, and inventory where it belongs and not out where clutter can trip employees or cause lost time in searches, etc.

As I mentioned above, not every entrepreneurship will require all five of those steps to their fullest extent. You'll notice, though, the five steps imply more than one person in the business. Let's talk about setting and hitting goals in this real business world when you don't have a partner by your side.

Chapter 8
You're Not in This Alone

Without devolving into social commentary, I will briefly state I'm aware many people today face life without a partner or a helpmate. You've read a few notes throughout this book that should make it no surprise to learn I not only divorced after thirteen years of marriage, but I also partnered with a predatory narcissist for several years. Neither individual was good for helping me pursue my career or my dream. I believe I've succeeded, despite their interference(s).

I share this to say, if you don't have a helpmate at your side — taking the trash to the curb on the correct day of the week so remembering that chore isn't taking up your brain space — you can still make it. You've got this if you believe.

> **It is through Jesus we have the strength to execute our goals.**

Yes, believe in yourself and in your dreams. But believe more in the saving Creator Who dwells within you and works all things for your good. I've talked quite a bit about perseverance and endurance so far in this book, but your perseverance isn't what determines success. The faithful reading this statement will understand what I mean when I explain; we can struggle, toil, and use up all our energy and still fail because we are nothing without Jesus Christ.

It is through Jesus we have the strength to execute our goals. We must remember to get out of our own way and let Jesus take the wheel. I could mix more metaphors in there, but you probably get it now.

That isn't to say we sit back and wait for Jesus to do all the work. You might have the Holy Spirit living within you, but you still must get out of bed in the morning, nourish yourself, respond to emails, order inventory, repair equipment, make the widgets, and so on. Those tasks might feel overwhelming at times, and you might long for a physical manifestation of help.

Books like the ones I mentioned in the introduction often remind us within their narrative there are clubs, organizations, non-profit associations, church groups, and community resources in every city where entrepreneurs can find support systems. You can reach out to professionals in your city/town for resources to assist in:

- learning new skills;
- sharing office space(s) and/or daycare service(s);
- creating co-marketing events;
- brainstorming product launches;
- planning community events;
- finding tax, payroll, or accounting advisors;
- joining mentor/mentee programs; and
- hundreds more activities directly or tangentially related to surviving alone while employed.

    I highly recommend starting with your preferred church group and the local chamber of commerce. Those two resources will be a foundation upon which the single human can build a strong system. I'm not suggesting you must get involved in the glee club. No, you don't need another extra-curricular activity when you're trying to work a day job, get a side hustle off the ground, maintain a second-hand vehicle, and prevent an apartment from crumbling inward on piles of laundry.

But as you develop friendships and business relationships within the community — that relational capital we introduced in chapter three — you'll find you're able to share some of the load. People who have lived in the community longer than you, or those who have a broader friends list than you, might be able to find short cuts or discounts for activities you hadn't thought of handing to anyone because of fees you believed would be cost-prohibitive.

For example:

- Maybe you can afford a discounted membership to a grocery delivery service to take that hour-per-week back for your schedule.
- Maybe you can carpool with a colleague (or two) to not only share fuel costs, but to also give yourself commute time for work on the side hustle while your co-pilot drives every other day.
- Maybe you can trade off babysitting with another single-parent entrepreneur once a week, so you're watching the kids while you're doing laundry and cleaning in whatever room they're playing games in. Combining chores with distraction frees you up to work on your side hustle spreadsheets or product development when the

kids are at your colleague's house. For no cost.
- Maybe you can share office rental with a set of colleagues from the chamber of commerce, so you not only have a safe snail mail address (read: a business address that's not your home), but you also have a space where you accomplish business web calls outside of a loud, roommate-filled apartment.

By sharing, bartering, trading, and working with other entrepreneurs in your community, you can save some costs and find yourself not alone. Even if you have a supportive partner in your life, you might find partnering with other entrepreneurs to be a useful tool in your toolbelt.

With the rise of AI, copious platforms exist to help you generate soulless emails that respond to people for you. At the 2024 Niche Media Conference, keynote speaker Andrew Davis, of NBC and *The Muppets* fame, walked us through the process of setting up your digital assistant.

More robust than a simple online avatar, this digital "twin" is your online helpmate, learning how to imitate your personal voice through inputs you provide it so it can answer emails, write marketing copy, prepare blog posts, and basically do anything else you don't want to pay a copywriter to do. For Andrew, that assistant is a time-saver, helping prepare and record promo spots for his upcoming speaking engagements.

I, personally, don't want an online entity learning how to mimic my tone and voice to fool the masses into thinking whatever it creates came from my brain. Instead, I'd like to have a clone take my car to the shop for maintenance and check the post office box on the way home while I write copy.

Because I *like* writing copy.

I enjoy the creative process. I don't want a digital assistant sending an email on my behalf to someone else's digital assistant. I want to know I'm talking to a human when I say, "Hey, which of the ideas did you implement from the article you read in *AsphaltPro*?" or "Hey, have you gotten into the advanced reader copy of my latest book yet?"

When you build a digital assistant, you feed it your own intellectual property. You use your own data and not that retrieved from other online sources (read: stolen), so the formation of that assistant shouldn't be construed as unethical. I don't want anyone to think I have a moral problem with the use of digital assistants.

My concern is the further distancing of human relationships.

Ed Wallace, whom we introduced in chapter three, spoke at the 2024 World of Asphalt's education sessions in Nashville on the importance of human relationships in business leadership. His subsequent article in *AsphaltPro* Magazine outlines for the audience how business leaders can use the elements he's noticed working with over two hundred and fifty companies to engage with the humans in your business, internally and externally. He wrote:

> "Most executives and managers will tell you that strong human relationships are critical to their success. They say they also need their team members and employees to be great at developing and maintaining relationships, collaborating, innovating, advocating for company goals, and keeping the organization functioning effectively. These leaders would say human relationships — as opposed to digital or what I like to call 'ethereal' relationships — are central to their ability to influence and inspire individuals to achieve their organization's mission. Whether it's external or internal business relationships, we need to understand how people think and act, what it takes for someone to want to listen to you, help you, work for you, work with you, and even buy from you."

In other words, Ed encourages the collaboration you'll see championed throughout this book via human relationships that can't be achieved through what he calls "improvisation or magic." While I'm oversimplifying his point, I call it "farming out the human connection to social media scheduling and machines."

There are still human virtual assistants available for hire, which you can find through outsourcing services or through specific industry working groups. For example, in the publishing industry, there are publishing virtual assistants who specialize in email marketing, fraud analysis, inbound sales, sales support, lead generation, data research, digital marketing, proofreading, and so on.

Those are real professionals performing services for a fee, assisting publishers, editors, circulation directors, and the sales team without you needing to hire full-time workers, which your new company might not be ready to do.

Once again, I encourage you to ask at your local chamber of commerce — or do a search online — for virtual assistants in your field of interest to see what's available and what level of help you can afford to bring into your goal at this time.

A colleague of mine who works out of her home in Columbia, Missouri built a side company, which assists in that type of connection and collaboration.

In 2015, Cara Owings, and her friend and business partner Jennifer Schenck, started Connection Exchange, which they describe on their website as, "a welcoming service that brings a gift to new business owners, general managers, and executive directors. We connect you to all our business community has to offer. This is a free service for all new business leaders or decision makers."

Cara described it as a welcome service for new businesses, new business owners, and also new homeowners, even though she and Jennifer started it as a way for entrepreneurs to gain a network right away in their area. She stated their purpose was to create mutually beneficial connections within the local community, allowing mentoring and collaboration with colleagues and vendors, while putting personal relationships back into the sales process.

The women built "welcome baskets" with information and products from local banks, marketing firms, and other businesses. These gifts are delivered to new businesses who sign up to receive them.

BLOCK TIME FOR THE SIDE HUSTLE
Cara and Jennifer didn't drop their day jobs to start Connection Exchange. The women pursued their side hustle alongside the regular jobs we've been talking about in this book — the jobs we possess to survive. Even though they enjoy what they do, the side hustle is a side passion and it's one they've turned into a success.

Cara explained they each put $50 of startup capital and many hours of sweat equity into Connection Exchange. And that's what a side passion takes. Cara shared she's chosen a day job that allows flexibility so she can accomplish her side hustle. Then she offered advice similar to what we saw from Bryce in chapter five.

"I time-block," Cara said. "I think you need good time-blocking skills. I also do tasks at night. This might not be for everyone, but I'm always connected to my phone. For example, my daughter and I are going to the pool after this interview, and I can take my phone and my laptop with me to get some work done there."

The women's hard work has paid off not only in the expansion of the business into multiple locations, but also in recognition. They were named one of Columbia Business Times' Top of the Town in 2016 and were a Columbia Chamber of Commerce Small Business of the Year Finalist in 2018. For 2019, they were named the City of Columbia, Missouri, Woman-Owned Business of the Year.

"We're delivering their info as a warm, fuzzy resource," Cara said. "We started it for businesses only, but in our second year, we started the ConnectS software package for the welcome service and added a residential side."

The women started Connection Exchange in their hometown of Columbia, Missouri, but now offer the model as a licensed business — similar to a franchise. "We have five total licensed locations. They get to use our best practices and our logo, and they get coaching from us."

- Columbia, MO area new resident
- Mid-Missouri area new business
- St. Charles County, St. Louis new business
- West County, St. Louis new business
- Boonslick, MO area

If you're in one of the business locations, you can reach out to your local Connection Exchange branch for information and "connections." If you're not in one of the business locations, you can visit your local chamber of commerce about who the leaders in your community are who might set it up. Maybe that's you! The website to visit is connection-exchange.com.

For me, I've found a great deal of help from the writing community online. No one's physically helping me drag the trash can to the curb while I get the dishes washed up, but there are members of the writing community who have been willing to share information, repost videos I've uploaded, and assist with finding answers rather than let me waste time on endless research. There are members of my inner circle to whom I can turn and say, "I need help finding a person in this field to write an introduction to a book."

Let's talk about this in the context of side collaborations for a moment. When I had a situation with my vehicle toward the end of 2023, a friend from Ziggy's Haven Bird Sanctuary in Inverness, Florida drove me (and my seizure-prone African grey parrot) to the university medical center in Gainesville. One of our conversations led to a business arrangement between her son and I for a line of candles and perfumes from the world of Onweald in my *Choices* fantasy series.

I'd been looking for someone to help me set up a line of fragrances for about five months at that point and her son had the perfect shop already online (at ShadowflameCreations.com). All we had to do was create customized scents and artwork. Now that's a reality and my readers can wear the perfume of my main character or the cologne of my dragon — they can burn the fragrances from my epic fantasy world.

Back when I was trying to publish a

companion parrot magazine on top of my other tasks, a freelance writer told me no one ever "made it big" on their own. She informed me I needed a partner to help me survive or I was going to fail at everything I was trying to do. That kind of negativity is a terrible thing to hear, and I want to make sure you, dear reader, hear a different message.

Yes, it's wonderful to have someone at your side who supports and defends you. It must be freeing to have someone pick up the dry cleaning after a business trip, take a box of books to donate to the library, fight with the local pharmacy to get a prescription filled, or what have you while you make equipment repairs to get your business ready for its upcoming week. It would be fantastic to have a helpmate fix dinner when you're in the middle of a productive brainstorming session you can't bring yourself to interrupt for something as mundane as food preparation.

> **Having a partner at your side isn't integral to your success. You've got this!**

Having that extra person in your life is not integral to your success.

Having a person physically in your life is not the secret to "making it big," as that freelancer said to me. Because she had multiple examples of entrepreneurs with partners who handled ordinary life tasks for them, she made a compelling case. But the truth of the matter is you can build a community of persons with the skills and the knowledge to assist.

And you can set your schedule to keep your life together, as I have done, until you reach a point where you can afford to hire a lawn care service to show up twice a month during the rainy season and do the lengthy task of keeping the neighbors from calling your local code enforcement about your yard while you map out next quarter's growth plan. Or while you handle the day job to afford the side hustle.

You can embrace the dragon of doing it on your own.

Please understand me: I fully support the idea of collaboration (as evidenced in the anecdotes throughout this book). I would never discourage the idea of working alongside other entrepreneurs, professionals, creatives, or what have you. During the ten-year anniversary of the Imaginarium Convention in Louisville, Kentucky, I interviewed Imaginator Guest Dacre Stoker. He is the poster child for creative collaboration.

From his graphic novel adaptations of his great grand-uncle's short stories to an upcoming documentary, *Bram Stoker: The Father of Dracula*, Dacre has worked with other writers, illustrators, magazine editors, anthology editors, historians, film producers, and tour guides, to name a few. His credits often list him as co-author and co-editor on projects because he knows how to work with credible and skilled professionals to bring a project to fruition.

Sharing the work with someone who brings their set of skills to the table is smart business, and I recommend studying Dacre to see this in action. You can watch an interview about those, and many vampiric, topics posted on the SandySaysRead channel on May 9, 2024.

Whatever you must do to make your dream happen, I believe in you. Not because I "have" to, but because you've made it this far in the book. If you have this level of perseverance and determination to learn what you can from me, then you're well on your way to making the dream come true in the real world.

I also want to remind the faithful among my readers we have a Savior who never leaves us. I can't count the number of nights I've collapsed and the only energy or brain power I had left in me was used to mutter a simple, "Please, help me," for my nightly prayer. The answer was a sense of relaxation washing over my pent-up muscles.

God never fails me, and He's not going to fail you, either. When we call on Him for guidance, strength, support, emotional healing, or whatever we need in the moment, He's listening. We might not always like the answer to slow down, to redirect, or whatever it is He's asking of us, but the sense of peace that settles me reminds me to reach out in my nightly prayers.

You'll notice quite a few of my examples or anecdotes mention exhaustion and late nights. I don't want to imply you must work yourself into a frenzy to achieve goals in today's business world. I'm probably not as good at time-management as I think I am. Thus, when I get to the end of the evening's to-do list, and it's after 10:00 p.m., I'm tired. I've worked myself into a state of anxiety over "getting everything done so I can get to sleep at a reasonable hour."

A person doesn't have to work 24/7 to be a success, although a person needs to be committed to the goal. You'll find there are times when it's necessary to forego a couple hours of sleep to complete a project that's on deadline. If you aren't willing to sacrifice occasionally, it's time to reevaluate how important the dream is.

Personally, I've spent many nights awake into the wee hours because the side hustle is that important to me. If the only time to finish editing a book is from 9:00 p.m. to 3:00 a.m., well, then, guess what I'm doing from 9:00 p.m. to 3:00 a.m.? If that's what it takes for this dream, that's what I'm willing to do.

When being interviewed for his autobiography, *In the Pleasure Groove: Love, Death & Duran Duran*, John Taylor listed the impressive accomplishments of his band in 1981. During that year, Duran Duran released their first album, went on three British tours, went to America for the first time, and wrote half the songs for their next album, *Rio*.

"We worked so hard," he told the interviewer of his reminiscing. "That's really what struck me was how much work we did. It takes away that sense of 'oh, you guys were so lucky.' We just worked really freaking hard. We were really driven and never took our foot off the accelerator pedal."

He pointed out the dream of making it big was something he and best friend Nick Rhodes considered "perfectly doable." They set goals and they met goals. "You set your first target," John said.

Now, John also spoke about the concept of burnout. As Bryce shared in chapter five, John acknowledged there can come a point where you've worked yourself too hard. "You just can't sustain that kind of momentum for four or five years I think it was," he said of the band's constant go-go-go.

Here's where I want to suggest, again, the dream doesn't have to happen overnight. Take advice from John and set your goals — your targets — like steppingstones to greatness.

I can offer tricks and tips to make the mundane tasks of this real life faster or easier, so there's more time for hitting goals. Call it time-management, if you like.

Put app blockers on your phone. Then, block gaming apps, notifications from social apps, and the like. I recommend deleting social media apps if you don't actively use them for marketing; but block notifications on your phone at the very least.

Learn how to time-block your Outlook or Gmail calendar so your email automatically sends a response that you're, "In the office using a chunk of productivity time and will respond to emails at such-n-such time later today" to keep email alerts from pinging you.

For those who require social media to assist in marketing and spreading the word about your product or your services, scheduling a slew of posts at the beginning of the month or quarter is a wise investment in time, but I want to offer a caution here.

A SOCIAL SCHEDULING CAUTION:
With today's ever-changing algorithms, different platforms and the people using them like to see the original poster (OP) engage with respondents to the scheduled post once it's up. Most schedulers, such as Buffer, eClincher, and HootSuite provide dashboards where you can monitor posts after they've gone live. Some schedulers allow you to respond without going to the platform and getting distracted by other conversations that might not be relevant to your product, service, audience development, and so on.

Starting down the road of audience development and newsletter list growth would turn into a full book on its own, so we'll stop with the idea of using a scheduler to save you time. But use it wisely to engage your new friends and colleagues, who could very well be among new customers.

Something else I've found that helps keep me in the zone is appropriate background music. I recommend you curate a few playlists of music for focus, productivity, study, and motivation so you can quickly and easily bring one of them up for background brain stimulation while you work. By keeping yourself focused — no interruptions from pinging phones and emails — you can accomplish more in the time set for a project.

Let's also look at what you can do with your blocks of time on a day off to make upcoming workdays more efficient. I recommend planning your weekly grocery run with the next week's meals in mind. Then meal-prep on the weekends so you can stack up the week's meals in the fridge for quick-n-easy, mindless re-heating. That not only saves you a ton of time throughout the week, but it also frees up your brain and reduces daily anxiety over decision-making.

As strange as this might sound, consider your wardrobe. You might have heard how smart it is to purchase only garments that can be machine-washed at home. By avoiding dry-clean-only clothing, you avoid both the cost and hassle of running to the dry cleaners. Twice.

When I was a little kid, I had a spreadsheet (It was a big piece of butcher paper.) with my outfits planned out for the week. Each night before bed, I would consult the spreadsheet and lay out my clothes so the morning could go quickly. (It's probably something to unpack with a therapist.) Today, I line up my shirts along the bar in the closet so I can grab-n-go. But here's something interesting I learned from Peter Furler.

Peter is a founder and original lead singer for The Newsboys. A few years ago, he explained in an interview why you always see him in all-black clothing. It's a creativity thing.

By having only black jeans, black t-shirts, and black shoes for options each day, Peter wastes zero creative thought or time from his life wondering, *What am I wearing to the gig tonight?* or, *"What am I wearing to the church retreat today?"* He grabs the next clean shirt off the pile and moves on to an important task instead.

There's something brilliant in that kind of simplicity, and I'm slowly reducing my wardrobe to jeans and purple-hued tops, because I do all my marketing in purple. The process is slow because I must put on the professional persona when I get on a stage to talk to groups about writing and marketing. Or when I sit at the National Asphalt Pavement Association's sustainability committee meeting. But I'm whittling the wardrobe down thanks to Peter's angst-saving idea.

Let's stop now and put some of the concepts from this chapter into a checklist you can use. Not all of them will apply to you if you're seeking a job where you go to an office daily, but you can pick and choose the line items that make sense to keep in mind.

- Research a virtual assistant service you can afford to get started with.
- Consider creating a digital assistant that can help you draft emails, marketing copy, promo messages, and the like in your voice and from your own content.
- Use social media schedulers (wisely) to post your marketing and audience-development content online.
- List out your skills; then list what additional skills you need to acquire or look for in a partner/collaborator.

- Seek out resources at the chamber of commerce, community center, or other local connecting centers.
- Reach out to colleagues who could carpool or share other time-consuming activities with you.
- Select services you can afford now to take mundane, time-consuming chores off your plate, and free up your time to use your specialized skills pursuing your dreams.
- Meal prep on the weekend (or whatever day you have off prior to the start of a long run of busy days).
- Set aside blocks of time for tasks (time-blocking).
- Make a music-for-focus playlist.
- Remember to pray.

Chapter 9

Capture Dragons in the Real World

Let's try a couple of exercises to find and maintain motivation. We'll start by performing the over-used and extremely cliché trick of making my name into an acronym. This device works to remember key steps toward acquiring a specific job or capturing a dream. We're going to set goals, take action, stay up late, use good discernment, and yeet negativity.

    I borrowed the first of those from Daymond John. He spoke of his acronym SHARK during his keynote address at the National Asphalt Pavement Association's annual meeting in January 2024, sharing with the audience the importance of, first and foremost, writing down goals that you read every morning and night.

S IS FOR SET GOALS.
While I could have used Publisher Stephen Zimmer's recent, "Stay relentless!" for the "S" in my name, and I fully support that concept, I'm going to stress the importance of setting goals that you've researched and thought through.

One reason to set your goals is to check them against reality. Make sure the dragon you're reaching for is worth the time and the energy you're putting into it. Make sure it's a dream worthy of your skills, talents, and passion.

Make sure it's realistic, too.

I'm the last person to discourage an entrepreneur from chasing a dream, but I want to caution a person against throwing large sums of money at something that's not feasible. If you need to check with a financial advisor — or two — and prospects are dismal given physical, geographic, emotional, and other limitations, you might need to adjust the goals and dreams to something that won't drain you mentally, physically, psychologically, and so on.

Maybe reality is telling you to merely set the goal for a longer term. If your financial situation is such that a dream career move needs to happen twenty years from now rather than four years from now, that's a pretty long-term goal.

ARE YOU UP FOR IT?

A IS FOR ACTION.
Newton's First Law of Motion, or the Law of Inertia, teaches us a body in motion tends to stay in motion. Conversely, a body at rest tends to stay at rest. Behavior Analyst Chase Hughes teaches us we have pathways in our brains to form new habits and we must train those pathways over a series of days; he mentions twenty-one as the typical sweet spot to form a habit. When we put those concepts together, it makes sense that we want to take action and keep at it to meet goals.

Think of it as you're resetting your brain into a growth mindset. We have the ability to use self-care and good brain-health habits to effect change in our attitudes and motivations. By practicing gratitude, trying new experiences, and calming your mind with one of the playlists I suggested above or with breathing exercises, you can lift your mind out of stale routines. You can perk up and change a sluggish mindset to help yourself out of a pattern of rest.

If you find yourself having trouble clicking away from dopamine-providing reels on social media to dive into the time-block for your dream, maybe your dream needs revamping. (Or you need to remove the over-tempting app from your phone.)

If your body is at rest, it's going to take something motivational to get it up from rest. Your dragon should be motivating you! Let it! Get excited about it and get moving!

N IS FOR NIGHTTIME.
You could argue I stole this one from Tom MacDonald. Let me explain, starting with who Tom is and why he offers me motivation.

I have an eclectic music collection. The playlist for writing this book, for example, includes everything from Chopin to Kenny Rogers to Deco to AC/DC to Led Zeppelin to The Newsboys to the aforementioned Tom MacDonald and, of course, Duran Duran. What I'm saying is, I listen to just about anything.

Tom has been on my radar the past few years because he's an independent rap artist who has built his dream career out of nothing but desire. He put together a blueprint for other indie artists to follow and it's one that has made him a multi-millionaire selling his own music and merch out of his living room.

Christmas 2022, he released the song "Ghost," which he wrote for his girlfriend and videographer, Nova Rockafeller. When the news broke that his fans pushed the song to Number One on the Billboard charts, I burst into tears, not only in joy for the artist, but in a strange sense of relief and commiseration.

He'd proved an independent creative can beat the system.

It *is* possible to write your own music, record it yourself, film the video in your own studio, with your own team and your own equipment, and release all of that through your own channels; and have your own fanbase support you so fully that you overcome the obstacles the music industry throws in your path to stop you.

Couldn't the same happen for a lowly independent author struggling to put her name on the map?

Tom has shared, loudly, that when you see a mainstream artist sitting on a pile of money and billboard record plaques, you just have to grind harder to make it big. That means, when the successful artist who has a marketing team and host of co-writers and co-producers behind him is sleeping, you've got to be up late, grinding.

So, the "N" in Sandy is for nighttime. In fact, I'm typing this sentence at 10:59 p.m. on a Tuesday after putting in a ten-hour workday at the day job. And there are many miles to go before I sleep.

D IS FOR DISCERNMENT.
We've looked at the idea of building an inner circle of fellow entrepreneurs with whom you can barter services and trade skills, but you want to use good discernment when partnering with others. Beware of energy vampires.

I will admit another of my mistakes here for you to glean a lesson from. As an example, the freelance writer I mentioned who told me I'd fail without a partner supporting me was adept at taking an hour per phone call to over-discuss every mistake she believed I was making. Her ability to pick apart my sentences, misunderstand me, accuse me of believing things I didn't believe, and alter things I did believe was astounding. Most phone calls with

Beware of energy vampires.

her left me drained of energy and motivation, but I felt I needed her free labor. I can admit now I wasn't using good discernment.

Look carefully at who will be a helper to you, and to whom you can be a helper in return. It's a fact not every entrepreneur you encounter will be in a stage to help you. Some will be a stage or two behind you and will benefit from the information and encouragement you can offer. That's wonderful!

But do be cautious of those who are a stage behind you and merely eager for handouts or for someone to do the work for them rather than receive education or assistance. In other words, use good discernment to avoid losing time, money, or energy to those who have no desire to help themselves or you.

> **We can work toward those dreams together and you might be surprised what gifts you have to share with someone!**

Y IS FOR YEET NEGATIVITY.
If you've watched any of the videos on my BookTube channel, you'll immediately recognize my "voice" in this motivational

item. I fully believe there's enough negativity in the world that we as individuals don't need to add to it. Instead, we should practice positivity as often as we can. I'd like to encourage you to practice that positivity and optimism in pursuit of your best job or dream career.

Whichever realistic goals you've set for yourself, don't let self-doubt and self-deprecation seep in when you're setting up your action plans. Stay positive and stay on track. If the people in your inner circle feed you negative vibes, ignore their bad words or put those people in a time-out.

While it's wise to listen to constructive criticism and implement reasonable, well-meaning changes as much as possible, some people need to go on mute when their constructive criticism turns into mean-spirited or degrading talk. After you've discerned who is offering useful ideas, squash your ego and use those ideas while yeeting the ones from bad actors. Cling to the idea from Galatians that tells us, "Let us not be desirous of vain glory, provoking one another, envying one another." (KJV, 1958, Gal. 5:26)

As we've discussed earlier in this book, you want to set a goal that makes sense for you and your skill set(s), which might mean taking criticism or augmenting skills you already have. For me, I knew at a young age I wanted to write books. I wanted to write stories that introduced the characters in my head to readers.

As mentioned in chapter one, I augmented my skills with an English degree with an emphasis in communications. For the real world, I used that education in a career in magazine publishing, which has included newsletter and newspaper publishing and various creative publications. The English degree doesn't look, at first blush, like it should equate with a career in journalism or editing, does it? But it worked out perfectly. And it blended into the side hustle, otherwise known as "the dream."

Let's apply that to what you've been thinking about while reading this book.

If you're interested in a creative career, do you need a college degree for it? And what kind of degree do you think you'd need? Graphic designers might or might not require a four-year degree at a state university, where the first year is spent padding your education with science, women's studies, and foreign language credits. Remember: I'm not knocking a well-rounded education, which might include those subjects; I'm merely suggesting they might not be vital enough to spend two or three hundred dollars per credit on and delay getting to your specific dream.

I've noticed friends near my age returning to school to achieve a Master of Fine Arts in creative writing. Several years ago, I investigated that concept and found it incredibly expensive. I also realized I can cherry-pick specific classes I want to take from experts in publishing at conferences and online instead of locking myself into a single program with professors who might or might not be up to date on current publishing industry practices.

That concept is available to anyone seeking a career in a creative field. You want education and training from people who have mastered the craft so they might assist you in technique and skill-building, but you don't necessarily have to get that education and training from an elite university with thirty-thousand-dollar tuition. Per year. Plus supplies.

To decide which goal-pursuing path is right for you, maybe you need to assess your dragon score.

Chapter 10

Assess Your Dragon Score

For the main exercise of this chapter, we can divide your style of pursuing goals into four dragon types. Those are found in my fantasy world of Onweald. Each of the four species has characteristics that lend themselves to taking different, positive action, but my hope is you'll see a blend of dragon traits in your propensity for tackling goals.

Turn the page (or visit the Dragon Score page on the SandyLenderInk website) and let's embark on the quest to find your Dragon Score!

THE GIANT DRAGONS

The giant dragons include Stone-Crusher and Ice, who are the size of mountains."[1]

When they rise from the landscape, they block the stars with their mass. For one of those massive creatures to fly, great energy is expended and there is, as you can imagine, incredible disruption and breaking of trees during takeoff. They are the entities that see the big-picture, all-encompassing, world-saving dreams, and work on the large project from that vantage point.

To determine how much of the giant dragon you have in you, start by asking yourself the following questions:

1. What is the overarching goal or dream I'm aiming for?
2. Why is that goal or dream important to me or what about it appeals to me so greatly?
3. What do I look forward to most about achieving this goal or how do I believe I will feel once I've reached it?

With those thoughts germinating in your mind, let's assign a value to the giant dragon characteristics. On a scale of 1 to 10 (with 1 being not very accurate and 10 being true most of the time), write the value you would assign to each of these when evaluating the following statements:

- I am good at diving right in to assemble a child's toy or piece of furniture just by looking at its picture/illustration. Value: ___
- It frustrates me when people take time during a meeting reviewing steps and assigning tasks that all members of the team should understand intuitively. Value: ___
- I don't need a list when I go to the grocery or hardware stores because I know what a meal or a project requires without consulting a recipe or instructions. Value: ___
- I see clear and obvious end results awaiting me if I achieve my dream career or side hustle. Value: ___

Total Giant Dragon Score: _____

THE WARRIOR DRAGONS
The warrior dragons include Oath-Maker, Malachi, and Adele, who are the size of what we would consider a two-story house.*[2] They are winged, scaled, reptilian dragons with gem-shaped heads and the ability to breathe fire.

They accomplish shorter, quicker goals with immediate, visible results. I call these stepping-stone goals, and they fit perfectly in the concept of "chunking" or stacking your goals to reach the final one.

To determine how much of the warrior dragon you have in you, ask yourself the following questions:

1. What obstacles do I see between where I am now and my end goal?

    How do I perceive and approach those obstacles?

2. What are the skills I have and what are the skills I need to obtain to reach my end goal?

    How do I plan to gain or augment those skills?

3. How easily do I set and stick to timelines or deadlines?

With those thoughts germinating in

your mind, let's assign a value to the warrior dragon characteristics. On a scale of 1 to 10 (with 1 being not very often and 10 being almost all the time), write the value you would assign to each of these when evaluating the following statements:

- I look at details and minutiae, focusing on and appreciating the nuances of a production or program. Value: ___
- I like to create lists and check off tasks I've accomplished as I do them. Value: ___
- I'm good at putting my tasks in order each day (or each week) so I can do my chores in a logical fashion and without frustration. Value: ___
- I see clear and obvious steps I'll need to take to stack my goals. Value: ___

Total Warrior Dragon Score: _____

THE SHOULDER DRAGONS
The shoulder dragons include Strike, Flame, and Glimmer, who are the size of a pet cat.[3] They are winged, adorable creatures with prehensile scaled tails.

When they gather, they're called a smoulder and they are supportive, guiding companions to humans they select. They fit perfectly into the category of someone who collaborates with and supports others on a dream journey.

To determine how much of the shoulder dragon you have in you, ask yourself the following questions:

1. Who do I know to fill in the skills I lack and help me toward my goal? How comfortable am I in reaching out to those people for their help?

2. Who can I reach out to if an obstacle becomes insurmountable? How will I react if I see an obstacle rising?

3. How comfortable am I working in a team or group environment where I mentor or assist others?

With those thoughts germinating in your mind, let's assign a value to the shoulder dragon characteristics. On a scale of 1 to 10 (with 1 being typically false and 10 being always true), write the value you would assign to each of these when evaluating the following statements:

- I enjoy working in groups. Value: ___
- I look for ways to mentor others. Value: ___
- I have no problem asking others for help. Value: ___
- I see clear and obvious ways my dream needs extra skills added to it — and some of those skills I don't yet possess. Value: ___

Total Shoulder Dragon Score: ____

THE WATER DRAGONS
The water dragons include those who are the size of what we would consider a commercial cruise ship and those whom we would consider the size of a speedboat.*4

They live in the five oceans of Onweald and represent the type of dreamer who is in it for the long haul — the dreamer who knows you must keep treading water to keep your head above the surface and must keep swimming to get to the shore.

I thank Stephen Zimmer for reminding me of Bruce Lee's philosophy here: Water changes to form to new obstacles as they arise, often reshaping the landscape as it adapts. Like the water, my water dragons flow and change to find solutions to problems as they arise.

To determine how much of the water dragon you have in you, ask yourself the following questions:

1. What potential challenges or obstacles will I need to adjust to?
2. What coping mechanisms do I have in place for restarting or pivoting during my journey?
3. How will I react to setbacks and changes?

With those thoughts germinating in your mind, let's assign a value to the water dragon characteristics. On a scale of 1 to 10 (with 1 being typically false and 10 being always true), write the value you would assign to each of these when evaluating the following statements:

- When there's a roadblock on my way to work (or an appointment), it's no problem for me to take a detour; it doesn't ruin my day or cause big angst. Value: ___
- I've experienced a job loss (or a failing grade) in the past and overcome it by learning a new skill, applying for a new job, re-taking the difficult course/subject, or some other action. Value: ___
- When people let me down, I can forgive them without getting angry, but I am more cautious about working with them or counting on them in the future. Value: ___
- I can see clear and obvious ways to approach the long-term goals that will get me to my dream career. Value: ___

Total Water Dragon Score: _____

Keeping in mind you are probably a combination of the four dragon types, let's look at your scores. If you notice you're handing yourself a score of twenty points in each of the categories, please go back and reflect on the statements again. You don't want to take the easy way out of assigning a middle "five" on all the statements.

If you have twenty or fewer points in a category, I want you to think of that dragon type as "lurking" in your personality. Its traits and characteristics are still available to you, but not as much a part of your natural state as some others.

If you have twenty-one to thirty points in a category, I want you to think of that dragon type as "rising" in your personality. Its traits and characteristics help you more often than you might realize. You can call on those soft skills at will.

If you have thirty-one to forty points in a category, that is your natural dragon type. Its traits and characteristics are what you call upon day in and day out to get through life, pursue dreams, and reach for new goals.

I hope you skew toward thirty or more points in at least one of the categories to showcase a decided strength in that area. Hopefully you lean toward being one of the dragon types with additional strengths in other types. For example, I'm a solid warrior dragon with the water and shoulder dragons rising and the giant dragon lurking.

> **I embody a recent social media meme: I failed as a Disney princess and became a dragon instead.**

Those dragon types all have the advantage of being malleable. Especially the water dragon! As you add to your skill set and accomplish the goals you're stacking toward the big, fabulous dream goal, you'll be adding to and augmenting the traits and characteristics that the "dragons" in your inner circle possess.

If you should find a step along the path becomes more intriguing than you thought it would, make sure you leave room to pursue that step further. Make sure you give yourself room to change direction, if you wish. Let's look next at giving ourselves grace to pivot along this journey.

Chapter 11

Give Yourself Permission to Pivot

Remember, in chapter five, Bryce spoke of shifting from one business opportunity to another as novel puzzles appeared. When he sees a problem in the paving industry, he works on a solution. If that leads to a new business venture, he considers whether it requires moving into that new opportunity. As outlined in his chapter, pivoting has offered lucrative outcomes.

You can apply the concept of pivoting to your full-time career, to your side-hustle dream, to the mini goals you stack up along the way, and so on.

Here's a non-financial and non-business example I can offer from my experience. I don't remember now what spurred my desire, but playing the violin caught my creative eye when I was signing up for electives way back in sixth grade. Of course, the school contacted my parents to ensure I had the necessary equipment — that would be a musical instrument — and my devious plan to secretly join the school orchestra was immediately quashed. My family didn't have the money in 1980 to spend on a violin — an instrument in which I might or might not retain interest.

Fast forward a year, and it's time to sign up for seventh grade classes. I still wanted to do the orchestra thing.

My parents caved and rented a violin for me. I joined the junior high orchestra, started taking private lessons, and soon the director told my folks to buy a quality violin for me. That became an absolute joy, and I graduated to a different private teacher who secured for me a seat in the community college orchestra.

Here's where things derail, and the idea of pivoting comes into play.

> **You can pivot if your goals aren't bringing you joy. You can choose another dream to pursue.**

Before my ninth-grade year, we moved from that school district to one that didn't have an orchestra program. No more support for the violin. I needed a different private teacher in the new city, and Mrs. Connelly was the wonderful lady we found. She helped me prepare a single Vivaldi piece for a competition for what seemed like a year.

I practiced that piece for months on end, memorizing each note."[1] The sad thing is, my passion for the instrument died away with that work. I still miss it. I took up the flute to play in the band my freshman year, and that went well.

Here's my point:

- You can practice something overmuch and become bored with it.
- You can practice something you don't particularly care for and become mediocre at best.
- You can practice something you despise and ruin your mental health.
- You can practice something until it's time to either put all that passion into motion or pivot and practice something else.

Does that last bullet point make sense? I want to impress upon you it's acceptable to change lanes. It's not the end of the world to realize something isn't bringing you the joy you once thought it would, or that it once did.

I mentioned earlier in the book, I had to admit when the companion parrot magazine had come to a point of financial failure. When I could no longer prepare the content and layout, sell ads and force advertisers to pay the invoices I repeatedly sent them, fight with the post office and printer over constant mail delivery problems, and pay from my personal income the difference between generated revenue and print and mailing costs, I had to make the gut-wrenching decision to close the publication. Keep in mind, I was publishing that magazine while employed full-time for *AsphaltPro*, which was and remains my first responsibility.

Did I cry over that decision? More than you know. I reversed subscription charges and returned voided checks to readers, all while receiving hateful, vicious messages from potential advertisers, bird stores that wanted to carry the magazine, and subscribers who didn't want a refund, but wanted the publication they'd signed up for.

> **You can pivot at any point along the journey to achieving the dream. There are more dragons to seek and acquire!**

It was a dark, depressing time. But it was necessary to pivot out of the workload and financial burden it was placing on me. My goal was no longer to grow a companion parrot magazine for spiteful, rude people. My goal was to retrieve my mental health and refocus my side-hustle energy on my first love — writing books.

Since recovering from the almost six-year companion parrot magazine debacle, I have achieved a variety of goals I've set for my author career and that, my reader, is a great feeling. After each achievement, we reach for the next goal on the list.

When ArcheBooks Publishing closed its doors in 2019, rather than view that as a setback, I sought a new publisher in Seventh Star Press and my *Choices* Series was remastered and re-released in June 2023. Finally, my first novel, *Choices Meant for Gods*, received an award from Shelf Unbound Media.

Other novels, novellas, and technical articles in *AsphaltPro* have won accolades, and I was honored to receive the 2023 Michael Knost Wings Award for my writing. While I consider that a huge honor, I'm not resting.

> **After each achievement, we reach for the next goal on the list.**

There are more goals to conquer! For instance, I've yet to meet the producer who will turn my epic fantasy series — or my young adult *Dragons in Space* Series — into a set of major motion pictures to thrill and amaze the masses. But I'm headed in that direction.

I've included those highlights at the culmination of this book's ideas not to brag, but to point out a solemn truth: You can do this, too.

If I can hold a full-time career — albeit sporadically — in the real world, escape an unsafe relationship, and overcome a financially and emotionally draining publishing side quest while pursuing the dream career as an author, then you, too, can thrive while reaching for your goals.

Please use the examples in this chapter to remember it's okay to modify a goal. If a job is bringing you anxiety and despair, there are ways to leave that stressful dragon behind and find a new one to be your champion. It is my hope some of the examples and points discussed throughout this book help you in either nurturing the good dragons or slaying the monsters in your career going forward.

> **Choose and nurture the good dragons that can help in your career going forward.**

Please use the ideas presented herein for setting realistic and achievable goals. Also recognize how your skills will influence your success.

You can build a business plan or a

career trajectory based on dreams and passion, and putting realistic goals based on skills you possess — or those you can learn — into place will help you fulfill the plan or take off on the path you want to pursue. Let the ideas that spark excitement within you fuel the plans you make, and you'll find a way to partner with the safe and serious entrepreneurs in your community and online who are as excited as you are to bring it all to fruition.

As we discussed throughout the book, there are entities out there willing to help: some for a fee, some for barter and trade, some as part of a chamber of commerce's free services. Lean on your personal Savior for hope and help in the low times and the high, to see how He's working for your good.

Whether or not you have a partner at your side, find and build your inner circle for your best chance at hitting every mini goal as you stack them toward success. Lean into your dragon type based on your dragon score and use those traits and characteristics to pursue what's going to bring you joy.

I wish you only the best in whichever path(s) you take. When you get to the lair, I hope *your* perfect dragon wins today!

**TAKE YOUR EXPERIENCE ONLINE AND
SHARE A DREAM WITH OTHERS.**

Use the Amazon or Goodreads platforms to share your dragon score and a goal you set for yourself while reading this book. Let the real-world business community encourage you, while you encourage others in that sphere. I would also be honored if you rate the book or include a review while you're there engaging with others. Thank you for reading, and all best wishes for your success!

NOTES

Chapter 2

*1
During a marketing education session, ArcheBooks Publishing Company Publisher Bob Gelinas told his authors the story of Author Tom Clancy's lottery winning event. Clancy had submitted *The Hunt for Red October* to the Navy Press, which, at the time, accepted two fiction manuscripts per year for publication. His was accepted and published, and a ranking member of the Navy, while accompanying then-President Ronald Reagan, finished reading the book while on Marine One. He handed it over as a recommended read. Thus, Reagan had it in his hand while walking across the White House lawn. A reporter from the press pool called out, "What are you reading?" Reagan called back with the title, author, and "It's a good book!" The rest is history. That's a lottery-winning event for an author.

*2
Issue #14 of *Oh Reader* Magazine stated there are over 1,300 books released in North America each day.

*3
Northeast Missouri State University,

Kirksville, Missouri changed its name to Truman State University in 1996. Additionally, I never received confirmation of the completed degrees my ex-husband received from the universities he attended, but I feel secure stating the political science degree was awarded to him based on the work he put in for it. That is not a conversation to expand upon in a business book.

Chapter 3

*1
I might be mis-remembering the number of programs lower than the actual. The point is J— would've had to have gone back to the vendor with a new layout and have them reprinted, in a rush, at great expense. That would've triggered an explosion from the boss, who was already fabricating much fault with him.

*2
The Center for Construction Research and Training (CPWR) stated in 2022, the construction industry's "workers accounted for 19.9% of all on-the-job fatal injuries but only 7.5% of employment."

*3
The statistics as of 2024 show up to 15% of the construction industry at large is now female; when you get into regional markets, the percentage drops to around 5%. *Sources: US Department of Labor* and

Stephens College, Columbia, Missouri.

Chapter 4

*1
A.J. Ronyak currently holds two United States patents. The first issued October 8, 2002, for his Hydrocarbonaceous Composition Containing Odor Suppressant is Patent US 6,461,421 B1. The second, issued January 17, 2006, for his Hydrocarbonaceous Composition is Patent US 6,987,201 B1. Canadian Patent 2,391,172 for Hydrocarbonaceous Composition Containing Odor Suppressant was granted and issued on April 7, 2009. The European Patent Specification EP 1,235,768 B1, for his Hydrocarbonaceous Composition Containing Odor Suppressant was issued March 16, 2005.

*2
The Construction Innovation Forum is a grass roots, non-profit organization. In 2004, the CIF chairman, Larry P. Jedele, P.E., wrote, "The sole purpose of CIF is [to] identify innovative techniques and methods that are proven to be effective in reducing construction costs, and improving quality, productivity and safety. This year marks our 15th anniversary. In that brief time, CIF has honored over 50 innovations from 20 different nations and evaluated hundreds more." CIF bestows the NOVA award on innovators and

inventors annually.

*3
Casey Waid, development officer of Auburn University's Samuel Ginn College of Engineering, Auburn, Alabama, shared the university plans to bestow more of these honorary alumni status awards on an annual basis, to highlight people who have contributed to the industry. A.J. received the first in the fall 2024. A.J. graduated from Gilmour Academy, Gates Mills, Ohio, in 1978, and obtained his degree in graphic design from The Art Institute of Atlanta in 1980.

Chapter 6
*1
The magazine's editor-in-chief, Ed Bible, resigned his post at the American Hereford Association to work at the American Angus Association's *Angus Journal*, headquartered in St. Joseph, Missouri, telling me on his way out he advised finding a new place "soon." Ed was a class act, and I trusted him. I began my job search and had begun my position at Group Three Communications when a former co-worker called to tell me of Ed's unexpected passing. He was a good man, a good boss, and a good person. I remember how he would join the staff at even the most mundane of tasks if we had a harsh deadline to meet. He didn't hide in his corner office while the rest of us toiled

into the night, but pitched in to do what he had the skill to do.

Chapter 7
*1
I was first introduced to the concept of SWOT with regard to assessing strengths, weaknesses, opportunities, and threats to an individual in the mental health conversation in Dr. Vince Hafeli's inaugural book titled *Mental Health and Suicide: My personal story and the story of those left behind, with a deep dive into the construction industry.* He's a champion for this topic. The SWOT assessment applies to analyzing entire corporations, as well.

Chapter 10
*1
The giant dragons mentioned here appear in my YA fantasy novel *Move the Stars*, which was released in 2020.

*2
The warrior dragons mentioned here appear throughout the *Choices* epic fantasy series, which was re-released by Seventh Star Press in 2023.

*3
The shoulder dragons mentioned here appear in my YA fantasy novel *Move the Stars*, which was released in 2020.

*4
The water dragons mentioned here appear in the world of Onweald, which houses my *Choices* series. Those dragons interact with characters from the *Choices* epic fantasy series in an upcoming novel.

Chapter 11

*1
I can still play the beginning of *Concerto in A Minor* from memory, even though I can no longer "play the violin." If you hand me the instrument and a bow, I can start that piece.

An Extra Note About Diffusing Your "Why"

In 1962, Everett Rogers authored *Diffusion of Innovations*. In his book, he illustrated a bell curve in which the first 16% of entrepreneurs and investors fall into the categories of innovators (2.5%) and early adopters (13.5%).

Presenters over the decades have since massaged the bell curve and determined the first 10% of those thought leaders are "easy" to capture but it's the first 20% of people you want to convince to buy into your new idea. You want 20% of the marketplace to reach what's called a tipping point. Are you seeking the tipping point toward success with your dream? If so, we have some goal-setting and dragon-pursuing to do with this book.

One way to bridge the 10% gap between the easily captured and the tipping point is to share your "why" with your marketplace. You can set up a strategy for what your overarching goal is and how you want to accomplish the main goal, but at the heart of it all is why.

While it is vital to express to potential customers how your product or service is meeting their need or solving their pain point, your story is of value to them as well. Humans will naturally connect with someone who has their heart invested in their business. Are you pursuing a dream because a grandparent stoked the interest in you? Share that. That's your "why" and it will resonate with potential clients. Your "why" will also guide you as you set your stackable goals toward the overarching dream.

Your "why" will resonate with your audience.

ABOUT THE AUTHOR

Sandy Lender is a bestselling poet and award-winning author of fantasy, literary fiction, poetry, and short story works. She's a construction magazine editor by day and author of #girlpower fantasy novels by night. She lives in Florida where she volunteers in sea turtle conservation and parrot rescue.

With a four-year degree in English and three-decade career in publishing, Sandy brings an understanding of public relations and journalism to a variety of projects. Her successes include traditionally and self-published novels, hundreds of articles, multiple short stories and poems in anthologies, a handful of technical and green writing awards, a 2020 Pushcart Prize nomination, a handful of literary awards, and the 2023 Michael Knost Wings award.

Her public speaking appearances include CONEXPO-CON/AGG 2011 and 2023, World of Asphalt, the Rocky Mountain Asphalt Conference and Expo, American Federation of Aviculture, various library talks, various writers' groups including the Naples Press Club and Gulf Coast Writers, Archon34 in St. Louis, Context in Ohio, Imaginarium in Kentucky, and more.

Subscribe to her free author newsletter at bit.ly/SSReNews. Her website is SandyLenderInk.com and her Amazon author page is listed as Sandy Lender.

OTHER WORKS BY SANDY LENDER

The Choices Series

The Dragons in Space Series

The Faerie Holidays Series

The Gentle Dragons Series

How to Train Your Human: A Guide for Parrots

...and many others

www.ingramcontent.com/pod-product-compliance
Lightning Source LLC
Chambersburg PA
CBHW071117160426
43196CB00013B/2600